"...your *extraordinary* work about the birth of the Citizens party...was well worth my time."

"You have lucidly dealt with a subject everyone else has neglected. I learned a lot about this business from your interviews. There were some fairly *astonishing* admissions in them. I admire you for taking on so unpopular a subject and hope the book strikes a chord among our peers."

"It is a substantial piece of work...it raises legitimate questions about the role of media in politics."

TV reporter to Citizens party candidate Barry Commoner during the 1980 presidential campaign: "Are you a serious candidate or are you just running on the issues?"...

*Life Magazine 1980*
Special Year End Issue

*"BULLSHIT!"*

*The Media
as
Power Brokers
in
Presidential
Elections*

*by
Jeffrey Gale*

Grateful acknowledgment is made for permission to reprint excerpts from: "Quotes of the Year," *Life* Magazine, 1980 Special Year-end Issue; *The Other Candidates: Third Parties in Presidential Elections*, University Press of New England, 1983, by Frank Smallwood; *The Real Campaign: How the Media Missed the Story of the 1980 Campaign*, Summit Books, 1982, by Jeff Greenfield; "Media as Massage," *Socialist Review* No. 56 (Vol. II, No. 2) March/April 1981, p. 64-65, by Todd Gitlin; "Political Ad's Vulgarity Defines the Campaign" Op-ed column, *Los Angeles Times* 10/8/80; "Citizens Party Born in Unorthodox Way" *New York Times*, 4/12/80 by Warren Weaver, Jr.; An Interview with Barry Commoner, *Rolling Stone* 5/1/80, p. 44-48, by Lawrence Weschler; Presidential Election Results, *Parade Magazine*, 7/19/81; "Rules of the Game" Part 4: "Is There a Better Way?" *Rolling Stone*, 11/13/80, by Alexander Cockburn and James Ridgeway; "Reduce the Military Budget" says Commoner of the Citizens party, *New York Times*, 5/30/82; "Talking to a Mule" *Columbia Journalism Review*, January/February 1981, p. 30-31, by Barry Commoner; "Survey Shows Concern by Public for Press Fairness" *New York Times*, 10/25/81, by Dierdre Carmody; An Interview with Barry Commoner, "The Solar Answer" *Suburbia Today, Gannett Westchester Rockland Newspaper*, 5/10/81, p. 7-9, by Loren Stell; "Citizens Party" *Progressive*, October, 1982, p. 36-38, by Marty Jezer; Green Party Inspires U.S. Environmentalists, *Whole Life Times*, June, 1983; The Significant Alternatives, *Progressive*, 1984, by Sidney Lens; Let a Black Democrat Run for President, *Washington Post*, 1983, by Jesse L. Jackson; Johnson, Clark Plea for Third Party Presidential Presence for 1984, *Citizens Voice*, 9/4/83; President's Popular Vote Lead Second Biggest in History, Official Tallies Show, Washington, D.C., 12/21/84, Associated Press.

Excerpts from this book were first published in *feed/back*, the *California Journalism Review* (Summer, 1982).
This manuscript was also accepted into a special archive at the University of Kansas in Lawrence, Kansas, which houses a complete history of alternative political parties in the United States.

For information about this book write: Bold Hawk Press, P.O. Box 588, Palm Springs, CA 92263.

ISBN 0-9620243-0-9

Cover design by Willy Blumhoff, Blumhoff Design
Typesetting by Words & Deeds, Inc., Los Angeles
Printed by Delta Lithograph

Printed in the United States of America

*For all journalists who believe that the only thing constant in life is change.*

# CONTENTS

# Part II

# Part III

# Appendix

# Introduction

## by

## Jack Tapleshay, Editor

This powerful compendium of interviews, speeches, articles and political documents clearly delineates the role of the national news media which have become the key power brokers in U.S. presidential elections.

*"BULLSHIT!"* discloses the truth that any legitimate alternative party is doomed to back page coverage at best. More often, third parties are doomed to NO coverage, even though they fulfill all requirements, state by state, to be placed on the ballot and to receive matching funds from the government.

Journalist Gale tells:

- How the national news media make or break, not only candidates, but political parties, as well.
- How the national news media kept the new alternative American political party, the Citizens party, from getting off the ground, by refusing to inform the public of its presence.
- How press, radio and television influence and manipulate public opinion by providing or withholding information.
- How there is an ever-increasing conflict between the media's methods in covering political candidates and the fundamental democratic precept that all citizens have the right to facts, criticism, competing ideas and the views of all candidates.

- How the media picked the winners and losers in the 1980 and 1984 presidential elections without giving the public a chance to review the alternative choices.

Having been national press secretary in 1984 for Sonia Johnson, the Citizens party presidential candidate and the first woman in one hundred years to qualify for a presidential ballot, Gale chronicles his persistent but unsuccessful attempts to gain the media exposure essential to any campaign. Gale's interviews, with Alexander Cockburn of the *Nation*, Tom Wicker of the *New York Times* and Jack Nelson of the *Los Angeles Times*, demonstrate the awareness of key media figures of the frustrating media paradox: You do not get coverage unless you are newsworthy and you are not newsworthy until you have been covered. Previously, in 1980, Citizens party presidential candidate, Barry Commoner, resorted to the famous "Bullshit" radio commercial (the namesake of this book) and only then did he receive even minimal media attention; and that focused, not on his primary issue — nuclear proliferation and Three Mile Island — but on his use of what was termed a "barnyard expletive".

The unique format of Gale's acclaimed first book presents readers with contemporary comment by many of America's best known and most influential journalists. In fact, the list of contributors reads like a Who's Who in American Journalism.

Evidence of this book's importance is represented by endorsements from Bill Moyers of CBS News; Av Westin, executive producer of "20/20" and vice-president of ABC News; James Hoge, publisher of the *New York Daily News*; Hodding Carter, III, PBS and the *Wall Street Journal*; William Greider, national editor of *Rolling Stone* magazine; Edwin Diamond, professor of journalism at NYU and author of numerous books on media criticism; and Adam Hochschild, contributing editor to *Mother Jones* magazine, who wrote a special foreword for the book.

Part I explains how and why the Citizens party was formed on principles, not images; how its membership defines and directs party activity, rather than merely casting votes every four years. Gale discusses how, amidst high hopes and notable media attention, the Citizens party convened in Cleveland with names such as Julian

Bond, Studs Terkel, Robert Browne, and Richard Barnett highlighting the affair. The sincerity and optimism of those electing Barry Commoner as the 1980 Citizens party presidential candidate, is enhanced by the media coverage the convention received. Unfortunately, the media's enthusiasm ended there.

In Part II, Gale interviews journalists Alexander Cockburn, Tom Wicker and Jack Nelson, who respond to frank questioning as to why the media ignored a candidate whose party's platform dealt directly with the issues of the day. The responses are honest in revealing that the media has become a decision maker.

In Part III, Gale examines the Citizens party's new approach based on its four years of preparation for the 1984 election and how, in spite of choosing a newsworthy and well-qualified candidate — Sonia Johnson — the media remained unswayed. Detailed accounts bring the media's role in the political process to the forefront. Gale then summarizes the lessons learned and questions the state of national communications and its influence in determining "winners and losers" in the political arena by making the decision to cover only the two major political parties.

The media chooses to ignore important social, military, energy and environmental issues in the 1988 presidential election. Instead, candidate "character" issues, personality and sensationalized personal problems dominate the media coverage. *"BULLSHIT!" The Media as Power Brokers in Presidential Elections* is "must" reading for every American citizen, journalist and student of politics and journalism who cares about the status of the free electorate in the United States and how the media are destroying it.

# Foreword

## by

### Adam Hochschild
*Contributing Editor,*
Mother Jones *and Author of*
Half the Way Home: A Memoir of Father and Son
*(Viking; 1986)*

The emergence of the Citizens party in the 1980 election season was, in its way, an interesting and significant event in the history of American dissent. Like all such events outside the political mainstream, coverage of it in the nation's press was scanty and uneven. Hence I'm glad to see this collection of materials made available for those who wish to go back and look at that bit of history more closely.

Looking back on those events myself, as someone who participated in them in a minor way, I have two observations:

1) The very coming into existence of the Citizens party remains an exhilarating experience for those of us who were involved. It was a vivid demonstration to all the participants, especially those who attended the various national meetings and the national convention in Cleveland, that there was a nationwide community of activists who shared a similar vision of progressive, non-sectarian left politics. I don't think anyone quite realized this before, at least not in such a dramatic way. Although there were a few debates over parts of the platform, the remarkable thing was that a large and diverse group of people rather quickly agreed on one at all.

2) In hindsight, though, I think we made a mistake in running a candidate for president in 1980. Part of the mistake was innocent; at the time the decision was made, we did not know that John Anderson was going to run his own independent candidacy, and Anderson, despite his mainstream politics, took up whatever attention American voters — and the media — were willing to devote to a third party candidate that year.

The other part of the mistake was political bad judgment, of which I'm just as guilty as the other members of the Citizens party majority, which pushed for presidential candidacy. Knowing that the party had no remote chance of victory, the only rationale for running a candidate was to point out how little the two major parties differed from each other and how the nation needed to look to alternative politics. Well, the nation *did* need to look to alternative politics, and still does. But unfortunately 1980 was a year in which the two major party candidates had real and deep political differences between them, differences wider than any between major party candidates in a generation. Millions of Americans who have suffered under Reaganomics can attest to this, as can millions of people in many countries who fear the effects of his unprecedented military buildup. Carter had his flaws, but the differences between him and Reagan cannot be waved away as blithely as we did in 1980.

I still have hopes that the Citizens party, or some force like it, will someday emerge onto the American scene in a major way. It won't be an easy feat to pull off, and will probably take many state and local victories before it can successfully go national. But the need is clearly there. As the U.S. faces the prospect of years more of intervention and war preparations abroad, and more economic stagnation at home, the job of organizing a national movement that offers a real alternative to all this becomes essential.

# Preface

### From The Real Campaign: How the Media Missed the Story of the 1980 Campaign (*Summit Books; 1982*)

### by

### Jeff Greenfield

*(Special correspondent for ABC News "Nightline")*

A coalition of left-wing groups had formed a new political organization, the Citizens party, and had chosen prominent environmentalist Barry Commoner as its presidential candidate. LaDonna Harris, an active feminist and wife of Fred Harris, former senator from Oklahoma, was chosen as his running mate. The party offered a radical platform, calling for nationalization of the railroads, sharp controls, public representation on the boards of major corporations and huge slashes in the defense budget. Except for an occasional whimsical piece on the evening news or public television programs such as the "MacNeil-Lehrer Report" and "Bill Moyers Journals", no one was listening. So in mid-October, the Commoner campaign delivered this radio commercial to the national networks:

"Bullshit!" declares a man.

"What?" says a shocked woman.

"Carter, Reagan, and Anderson — it's all bullshit," the man replies, contending that only Barry Commoner is talking about what really needs to be done. The five thousand dollar media buy aroused hundreds of complaints and wails of anguish from local stations, but F.C.C. rules are clear: as long as a candidate's face or voice is on a commercial, absolutely no censorship is permitted....[However, in spite of the clear F.C.C. ruling, most local stations that previewed the commercial, chose not to run it because of fear of repercussions from the F.C.C.]. In an irony to which Commoner himself pointed throughout the rest of the campaign, this single radio commercial earned the Citizens party more free media than all of the months of campaigning, speeches and position papers put together. It also revealed the differing standards of the mainstream press about colorful language. *Time Magazine* used the word "bullshit," the *New York Times* called it a "barnyard expletive." CBS bleeped out the last half of the word and one radio station called the term "bovine excreta."

---

*Todd Gitlin, in "Media as Massage"*
*Campaign '80,*
Socialist Review,
*No. 56 (vol. II, No. 2), March-*
*April 1981, p. 64-65.*

The Citizens party knew just what it was doing with its famous 'Bullshit' commercial; that was the only moment in the campaign when it got any national coverage. On "Lights, Cameras, Politics," Walter Cronkite had told Richard Reeves: "We know who is serious and who is not serious; we know who has something to say to the American people, and who does not." Thus the media took John Anderson very seriously in the New Hampshire primary and there-after; they also tuned him down when the potent polls showed him dropping to *only* twelve percent or so. If Barry Commoner or Ed Clark had been a member of Congress, or otherwise entitled to the media

respect due an authoritative personage, he might have edged onto
the floodlit map. As it was, the small-party candidates had no chance
of being taken seriously.

*Todd Gitlin's latest book is The Sixties: Years of Hope, Days of Rage
(Bantam Books; 1987)*

---

## Lawrence Weschler
*(Staff Writer for the* New Yorker*) in
"Political Ad's Vulgarity Defines the
Campaign."*
*Op-ed column in* L.A. Times
*October 8, 1980*

On the afternoon of Tuesday, October 14, 1980, at 2:59, the
strangest thing began happening to the radio in my living room. I was
tuned to KNX-Newsradio, anticipating the *ping-ding-ding-dah-dah*
that always signals the onset of CBS' hourly national news. But
instead of the *ping*, a somber voice intervened, explaining earnestly
that at some point in the next five minutes a paid political announce-
ment would be broadcast that contained offensive language. CBS, the
voice said, disapproved of the language, but their lawyers had
advised them, after consultations with the Federal Communications
Commission, and in order to comply with the First Amendment, that
they would have to run the ad. They were sorry.

It sounded pretty intriguing; I kept my ears perked as the
newscast proceeded apace: Ronald Reagan would appoint a woman
to the Supreme Court; Jimmy Carter would change his campaign style
and be less abrasive, even though he felt that his opponent really
could get us into war but he wouldn't say so anymore; John Anderson
was talking to college students somewhere, and so on. Then there

was a moment's silence, followed by background sounds of a cocktail party. A male voice said, "Bullshit!" A female voice gasped, "What?" "Carter, Reagan, Anderson," the male voice explained, "It's too bad people have to use such strong language, but isn't that what you think too? That's why we started an entirely new political party, the Citizens party. The truth is, we've got to break the power of the corporations. Profit-oriented corporate decisions have left the rest of us with high inflation, nuclear insanity and a poisoned environment. Hello, I'm Barry Commoner, the Citizens party candidate for president..."

As soon as the ad ended, the same earnest voice came on, once again lavishing disclaimers and apologies to delouse the air. About half an hour later I called KNX and asked if they had been getting any objections to the ad, and the frazzled receptionist assured me that CBS affiliate stations around the country were being deluged. I decided to conduct my own totally unscientific random sample of public sensitivity, calling at random 20 telephone numbers, asking whoever picked up the phone to fill in the blank: The presidential election campaign so far has been mainly...Three people hung up, five used words like "boring," "confusing" and "exasperating" and 12 said "bullshit."

If the Commoner people were trying to draw attention to themselves, their ploy apparently worked. The evening news across all the networks was peppered with references to the ad. Discussion was pretty much confined to the language involved, not the message.

I found myself wondering about the state of affairs in a country where 12 out of 20 random individuals would use 'a barnyard epithet', (as Associated Press quaintly dubbed the phrase in its morning dispatch), to describe the campaign for the nation's highest office.

It's not as if people don't have specific concerns. It has been, after all, less than two years since the oil companies hiked the price of gasoline, reaping huge profits, while in New England some senior citizens were unable to afford heating oil. All the head of the Federal Reserve Bank could tell them was that Americans were going to have to resign themselves to a lower standard of living in hopes that the economy would come out of its tailspin. And it was only last year that the nuclear reactor at Three Mile Island came dangerously close to melting down. On the other side of the globe, the meltdown of the Shah's regime has given everyone a chance to assess the wisdom of some practices of American foreign policy that have prevailed since World War II. And yet, amazingly, none of this recent history has been seriously discussed in this year's presidential campaign. Instead, we have been inundated with talk of momentum, polls, vice-presidential sweepstakes, electoral counts, style and tone.

Several months back, when the League of Women Voters was trying to engineer its debates, Barry Commoner and the Citizens party argued that consideration of a candidate's standing in the polls was an inappropriate way of going about an election. Commoner pointed out that the Citizens party had qualified for the ballot in 30 states and therefore had a right to be included in any debate. More important, he argued that the debates should be *debates*, not public-relations panels but debates about issues (say, nuclear power one week, the state of America's auto industry the next, and so on), and that the full range of opinions and ideas needed to be aired. But that hasn't happened.

Is it any wonder that so many people, when assessing their political horizons, find themselves reduced to muttering barnyard blather?

*Lawrence Weschler is author of:* The Passion of Poland: From Solidarity to the State of War. *(Pantheon: 1981)*

# PART I

## *How and Why The Citizens Party Was Formed*

Summary: Explains how and why the Citizens party was formed; gives background information about the party's platform and organization, and reflects the spirit of the Citizens party national convention in April, 1980 — the only period the national media granted the party appropriate attention. Also included is "Sonia Who?", the article which describes the frustrating wall of silence the media created that prevented the Citizens party National Press Secretary, Jeffrey Gale, from getting the media coverage necessary to bring the new candidate before the American people.

# "Sonia Who?"
## by
## Jeffrey Gale

*"Your candidacy was a secret...just between*
*you and the media."*
*(from "Sonia" by Charlotte Taft)*

"Is this Walter Goodman, journalist on the metro desk of the *New York Times?*"

"Yes. Who is this?"

"Walter, my name is Jeffrey Gale. I'm a journalist and I have read the pieces you have written this fall about David Bergland, Dennis Serrette, and Lyndon LaRouche." (alternative party candidates for president.)

"I was just wondering if you had ever been assigned to interview the only woman running for the presidency on November 6...Sonia Johnson?"

"Sonia who?"

The above conversation did not take place as part of the late George Orwell's *1984.* It *was* "Newspeak," one week before the *Times* locked up another four years of presidential campaign reporting.

Goodman went on to say how he had also done a piece on Gus Hall, Communist party candidate for president, but would check with

David Jones, national news editor, to try to see why Irvin Horowitz, assistant editor of national news, Jones' assistant, had decided to kill Phil Gailey's in-depth interview with candidate Johnson.

This is the inside story of what it was like to serve as a national press secretary for the only woman who was running for president of the United States on November 6, 1984...Sonia Johnson.

Sonia Johnson was nominated to run for the presidency at the annual national convention of the Citizens party which was held on the campus of Hamlin College near St. Paul, Minnesota, on August 11, 1984. I first met Sonia Johnson during the long Labor Day weekend in San Francisco in 1983 at a national convention of the Citizens party. At that convention, Barry Commoner, who ran for president on the Citizens party ticket in 1980 with LaDonna Harris as his running mate, told the convention he felt that in 1984 the Citizens party should back the candidacy of the Rev. Jesse Jackson in the Democratic primaries. He felt that Jackson had basically the same beliefs that were set forth in the Citizens party platform at its nominating convention in Cleveland in April of 1980. At that convention, former U.S. Attorney General Ramsey Clark also endorsed Jackson's candidacy. Jackson had called in both Clark and Commoner for a private meeting prior to that Labor Day convention and word of that meeting had leaked to the *New York Times*. The *New York Times* ran an interview with Barry Commoner prior to the convention, and in the interview, Commoner stated that he had met with Jackson, had endorsed Jackson's candidacy, and had decided not to run for president again.

The delegates to the Citizens party convention in San Francisco took a vote and decided the reason the party had been founded to begin with was that they felt both the Democratic and Republican parties had failed to meet the needs of the nation; thus, the delegates overwhelmingly rejected Commoner's idea. Commoner packed his bags and went home to Brooklyn Heights shortly after the convention began. Sonia Johnson gave a major speech. She had been contacted by many people in the party and in the women's movement and was asked if she would consider running for president on the Citizens party ticket. In 1979, the year the Citizens party was founded by Dr. Commoner, Julian Bond, Bella Abzug, Studs Terkel, Adam

Hochschild, Ed Sadlowski, and others, Sonia Johnson, who had been a member of the Mormon Church throughout her lifetime, was excommunicated from that church because she supported passage of the Equal Rights Amendment for women. She had fasted on the steps of the state capitol in Springfield, Illinois for 37 days because the state of Illinois failed to ratify the equal rights amendment. Based on these experiences, Sonia Johnson signed a contract with Doubleday Publishing Company and wrote the widely-acclaimed book *From Housewife to Heretic.** Johnson had voted for Independent candidate John Anderson in 1980 and was not an active member of the Citizens party. In Minnesota, the Citizens party overwhelmingly nominated her to run and chose Richard Walton, journalist and author, to run with her for vice-president.

During the 1980 presidential campaign, I served as a voluntary ombudsman for the national news media on Commoner's candidacy. For many weeks, I personally contacted the national news media to suggest they give more coverage to Commoner's candidacy. Commoner had authored many books dealing with the environment. He had been on the cover of *Time* magazine twelve years before former-President James Earl Carter, Jr. made the cover of *Time*. However, Commoner was basically ignored by the national news media. Only a handful of journalists were able to get pieces published on Commoner: Alexander Cockburn, then with the *Village Voice*, along with his writing partner at that time, James Ridgeway, did a cover story for the *Village Voice* one week before the election and the *Village Voice* endorsed Barry Commoner for president of the United States. The *Voice*, the number one national weekly newspaper in the United States, in the 1984 campaign never once did an interview with Sonia Johnson. Between 1980 and 1984, Cockburn resigned from the *Village Voice*, but his writing partner, James Ridgeway, who had known Sonia Johnson for several years, met with Sonia, suggested that she not run and, despite my contacting him, he never once wrote

---

*Sonia Johnson, Author of: *From Housewife to Heretic* (Doubleday: 1981) *Going Out of Our Minds: The Metaphysics of Liberation* (The Crossing Press; 1987)

an article for the *Village Voice* during the 1984 presidential campaign on Sonia Johnson's candidacy.

In the 1980 campaign, Commoner qualified to be on 30 ballots. He received only 230,000 votes on election day which is about the size of the last major anti-nuke rally that was held in the New York City area. In 1980, John Anderson, who lost as a republican when he ran against Ronald Reagan and then decided to run as an independent, qualified for all 50 ballots. He garnered six million votes and also was granted six million dollars in matching funds by the taxpayers of the United States through the Federal government. Anderson, of course, decided not to run in 1984 and openly backed the candidacy of Walter Mondale, a democrat, for president of the United States. When Jackson did not do well in the primaries, Barry Commoner also stumped for Mondale. In 1980, the only other presidential candidate to qualify for all 50 ballots was Ed Clark, running as the presidential candidate of the Libertarian party which had also run a presidential candidate in 1976.

Because of Anderson's strong showing in 1980 when he managed to get major national media support, the rules were severely tightened by many states making it very difficult for alternative party candidates to qualify for the ballot. Therefore, in the 1984 presidential election, although 13 different candidates were running for president on November 6, 1984, in many of the 50 States, no candidate other than President Reagan or candidate Mondale qualified to be on all 50 ballots. David Bergland, who was the presidential nominee of the Libertarian party, only qualified to be on 39 ballots. Sonia Johnson qualified to be on 17 ballots but she was a write-in candidate in 10 other states.

Prior to the 1984 election, Sonia Johnson had been on every major talk show in the United States. Her book had been reviewed in most of the major newspapers and magazines and received outstanding reviews from most of them.

Johnson's strategy was based on one major factor: when she received the nomination, she decided that she would only run a campaign in the black. Commoner's candidacy had left the Citizens party deep in the red. Johnson's major goal was not to see how many votes she could get, but to have her voice heard and also to become the first alternative party candidate for president in American political history to qualify for matching funds from the federal government so as to enable her to run for the presidency. With a small, dedicated staff of volunteers from all over the country, Johnson managed to raise more than five thousand dollars in each of 20 States and thus qualified for matching funds from the federal government. When she did this, for the first time since her nomination, she managed to get the wire services to finally pay attention to her candidacy.

Her second major goal was to try to be included in any nationally televised presidential debates during the 1984 campaign. She hired attorney, John Armor, who had been the attorney, in 1976 for the former-U.S. Senator from Minnesota, Eugene McCarthy, and for the former-Governor of Mississippi, Lester Maddox. In 1980, the League of Women Voters told Anderson that because his rating in the polls had fallen below 20 percent, he would not be allowed in the only major presidential debate of that campaign, which was held in Cleveland one week before the election with President Carter and former-Governor of California, Ronald Reagan. At that time, Armor suggested that Anderson file a complaint with the Federal Communications Commission that would state that because of the debates in 1976 between former-President Gerald Ford and then-Governor of Georgia, Jimmy Carter, the debates had become an integral part of the electoral process.

Armor felt that no one could become president of the United States who was not allowed in a televised presidential debate. However, Anderson decided not to fight, and on that day, most people in the national news media, and the public, felt he threw in the towel and his candidacy was over.

Johnson decided to fight. Right after her nomination in August of 1984, she started her battle with the League of Women Voters and with the networks to be included in any nationally televised presidential debates. The League of Women Voters told her that she would not be allowed in the debates. Johnson said that was totally unfair because she had qualified for matching federal funds and was on the ballot in enough states to garner more than the necessary 270 electoral college votes to become president.

President Reagan and former-Vice-President Mondale both went on record, in 1984, stating they believed that the debates had become an integral part of the process. Armor then filed a complaint in the U.S. District Court of Appeals in Washington, D.C. Many legal experts and well-known national journalists felt that Johnson's would be a precedent-setting case. Johnson asked the Court to force the F.C.C. to uphold the right of alternative party candidates, who are on the ballot in enough states to garner more than 270 electoral college votes, to be included in any nationally televised debates with the republican and democratic nominees. The Court did not hear the case until October 21, 1985, long after the 1984 presidential election was over and did not hand down a decision until two years later in 1987 when the Court ruled against Johnson. As this book goes to press early in 1988, an appeal to the U.S. Supreme Court is being considered.[1]

When I was hired as Johnson's national press secretary on September 17, 1984, I decided that my first goal was to see if we could get the *New York Times* to do an in-depth personal interview with her. At the *New York Times* bureau in Washington I met with Philip Gailey, one of the top political correspondents in that bureau. Gailey scheduled an interview with Sonia and we brought her into his office several days later. He did an in-depth interview with her, with another *Times* correspondent present. Gailey filed the story to the national news desk in New York. Several weeks went by and after he talked to the Assistant National News Editor, Irvin Horowitz, he was informed that the interview that he did with Johnson would probably be killed because the *Times* had yet to publish interviews with many of the other 10 alternative party candidates who were seeking the presidency.

I cite this example to illustrate the attitude of the national news media toward alternative political party candidates in the United States in the election of 1984. Despite the fact that I brought this issue to the attention of Charlotte Curtis, associate editor of the *New York Times*; Tom Wicker, associate editor of the *New York Times* and "Punch" Sulzberger, *Times* publisher, the *Times* never ran Gailey's interview with Sonia Johnson. Sulzberger had written me a personal

---

[1] see Appendix II

7

letter about my book that dealt with how, in 1980, the national news media covered the birth of the new political party, the Citizens party. He said that he was so impressed with it that he passed it around to other key editors at the paper so that in the 1984 presidential election, the Citizens party would be given more adequate coverage.

When Sonia Johnson was nominated, the *New York Times* sent James Barron from the Detroit bureau to Minnesota to cover the convention. Prior to that, when Johnson decided to seek the nomination, the *Times* had run a major wire story about her decision to run for president.

On Sunday, November 4, it struck me that there were 13 national football league games in the United States, and that both major wire services had a journalist cover each one of these games. Yet on November 6, when there were only 13 candidates running for president of the United States, only two candidates, President Reagan and candidate Mondale, were assigned journalists to cover their campaigns. The attitude of other branches of the national news media filtered down, really, from the decision the *New York Times* had made. At no time during the 1980 campaign or the 1984 campaign were candidates Commoner or Johnson invited to be on nationally televised shows such as "Meet the Press," "Face the Nation," "Issues and Answers" or "This Week With David Brinkley."

The *Washington Post* ran a front page story by its television critic, Tom Shales, about the fact that Phil Donahue, the number-one-rated television talk show host, had invited presidential candidates and vice-presidential candidates to be on his show and that they had all declined other than Geraldine Ferraro, congressperson from the state of New York, who was nominated to run for vice-president with Mondale. Donahue had Barry Commoner on his show after the incident at Three Mile Island in 1979, and because of the tremendous positive feedback he had gotten from that show, Commoner decided to help found the Citizens party and eventually became its first presidential candidate. Donahue also had Sonia Johnson on his show in her role as author, after her book was published by Doubleday. However, many people in the Mormon Church had written Donahue and telephoned him to say how upset they were about that show.

After that, despite the numerous times I called and went to Donahue's office, he declined to interview Sonia Johnson on his show again, even though she was a presidential candidate. After I took the position as Johnson's national press secretary in 1984, I called Ben Bradlee, the Executive Editor of the *Washington Post* and reminded him of my 1980 interview with him for the purposes of research for this book. I asked him when the *Washington Post* would do an in-depth interview with Sonia Johnson. His attitude was much the same as that of the New York editors on the national news desk of the *New York Times*. He said, "Jeffrey, is it urgent?" The only major interview that the *Washington Post* did with Sonia Johnson was done because one journalist, T.R. Reid, of the Denver bureau, called Dan Balz, on the national news desk, and told Dan that he wanted to do an interview with Bergland and a separate interview with Johnson. Balz agreed and Reid left the Denver bureau and traveled to Detroit to do a very fine in-depth interview with Sonia Johnson.

I first met with Charlotte Saikowski who in the past had written editorials for the *Christian Science Monitor* and was then in charge of the Washington bureau. She said, "Jeffrey, we just don't have the manpower available; however, I will talk to some of my political reporters and see what can be done." The only piece that the *Monitor* did involving Sonia Johnson was by a journalist out of the Boston office via telephone. It was a wrap up about all eleven alternative party candidates who were seeking the presidency. Later I met with Richard Strout and John Dillin, both journalists with the *Monitor's* Washington bureau, and I called Godfrey Sperling, Jr., to see if any of them would be willing to either write a column or do a personal interview with Sonia Johnson, but no one ever did.

*USA Today,* a two-year-old national daily newspaper based in Arlington, Virginia, close to the home and office of Sonia Johnson, also refused to do an in-depth interview with her. However, they were the only national daily newspaper in the United States to allow her to write an editorial page column. On the morning of the first nationally televised presidential debate, they asked her to detail in four hundred words or less why she should have been included in that night's debate.

Charlotte Curtis' office suggested that I have Sonia write a similar piece of seven hundred words or less for the Op-ed page of the *New York Times*. However, Robert Semple and his staff never ran the piece that she wrote specifically for the *New York Times*. He said that the *Times* had too many Op-ed page columns dealing with the November 6 election and, unfortunately, despite Charlotte Curtis' suggestion, they would not be able to run it.

That same piece was then offered to Meg Greenfield, the Op-ed page editor of the *Washington Post* and she also declined to run the column.

Shortly after September 17, I contacted Albert Hunt, the Washington bureau chief of the *Wall Street Journal* and James Perry, one of the *Journal's* top political writers, about the possibility of the *Wall Street Journal* doing an in-depth interview with Sonia Johnson. During the 1980 presidential campaign, the *Wall Street Journal* was the only major national newspaper which never did an interview or article about Barry Commoner. Despite the fact that journalists Ellen Hume and Suzanne Garment were personally contacted, the *Wall Street Journal* in 1984, never did write one sentence about Sonia Johnson's candidacy. And in the last week of the campaign, Albert Hunt, Washington bureau chief of the *Wall Street Journal*, wrote a letter apologizing for the fact that, because time was so short, he personally could not write the interview himself, but that, in 1988, amends would be made.

During the 1980 presidential campaign, Barry Commoner only received coverage on the evening news shows during the last week of his campaign. He allowed the famous "Bullshit" commercial to be aired on national radio. This was done specifically to protest the fact that the national media had basically ignored his campaign and given Anderson tremendous coverage when Commoner was the real alternative in the election.

Also, Sonia Johnson was never once interviewed on the evening news during the 1984 campaign, although I was in contact with Dan Rather and Bill Moyers at CBS News, personally met with Tom Brokaw at NBC News and also contacted Peter Jennings at ABC News. Unlike the 1980 campaign, when nationally-known radio talk show hosts like Larry King and Michael Jackson interviewed Commoner several times, those talk show hosts told me in 1984 that they were not allowed to interview candidates who were seeking office. I also personally met with Studs Terkel, who had been one of the founders of the Citizens party and that was his attitude as well. He said he would be very happy to have Sonia Johnson on his show, but only after election day.

When I reflect on the events prior to November 6, 1984 I think what's even more disconcerting than the *New York Times* not covering the 1984 Sonia Johnson campaign, is how the alternative news media in broadcast journalism almost completely ignored the Sonia Johnson campaign.

For instance, when I took the position as Johnson's national press secretary, I immediately contacted Jim Lehrer, knowing that the "MacNeil-Lehrer News Hour" had expanded to 60 minutes from the 30 minute show they had during the 1980 presidential campaign. My key purpose was to have Charlayne Hunter Gault, who formerly was with the *New York Times*, or Judy Woodruff, along with Les Crystal and Robin MacNeil, who came over from NBC to do an in-depth interview in the expanded format with candidate Johnson. Although Lehrer, as well as each one of these people were contacted individually, along with Les Crystal, the executive producer of the show, the MacNeil-Lehrer News Hour declined to ever do an interview with Sonia Johnson.

As far as radio was concerned, National Public Radio took a similar attitude. When candidate Johnson officially declared her candidacy, Susan Stamberg had her on for about four-and-a-half minutes on "All Things Considered" one evening. However, during the rest of the campaign, the network had Sonia on only once when Linda Wertheimer did "All Things Considered", and that was during one segment of a Saturday show.

On the other hand, Ted Turner's Cable News Network, which was really a fledgling 24-hour-a-day news network during the 1980 campaign, played a much bigger role in 1984. Sonia Johnson was on that network's various shows half-a-dozen times and Sonia even had lunch with Ted Turner at one point later in the campaign.

Sonia was on C-Span, which is only seen on cable television nationally. However, after she was told by the League of Women

Voters that she wouldn't be allowed in either nationally-televised debate, we were hoping that C-Span would do what Cable News Network did for John Anderson in 1980 and allow Sonia to go back on C-Span and answer each question that President Reagan and candidate Mondale had been asked in each one of the debates. Then people from around the United States could ask Sonia questions as well. However, C-Span refused to have her on.

United Press International did several interviews with Sonia Johnson, and Mike Feinsilber, who had known Sonia for several years, did a couple of in-depth interviews for Associated Press during the campaign. The AP was the only national news media organization which showed up in front of the courthouse the day she filed what many believed would be a precedent-setting lawsuit.

During the 1980 presidential campaign, the *Los Angeles Times* had Lee May of its Washington bureau do a short piece about Barry Commoner. It later had Robert Scheer do an in-depth interview with Commoner, which was buried inside the paper and edited down to a very short piece. In 1984, after contacting Jack Nelson, Washington bureau chief of the *Los Angeles Times*, I was passed along to Richard Cooper, the national news editor. Cooper assigned Lee May to do an in-depth interview with Johnson. May went to Johnson's office in Arlington with a photographer and did his piece. However, when it was suggested that May be allowed to travel with her in California during the last week of the campaign, the national news desk in Los Angeles would not allow May to do this.

Dan Balz of the *Washington Post* was the only national news editor who allowed one of his journalists, Tom Reid, to actually follow Sonia Johnson on the campaign trail.

During the 1984 presidential campaign, the national news magazines also ignored Johnson's candidacy. One week before Election Day, *U.S. News and World Report* included Johnson in a piece which mentioned that over two hundred Americans had originally decided to run for the presidency in 1984, although only 13 qualified to actually be on ballots on November 6th.

Unlike 1980, when the alternative news organizations gave major coverage to Commoner, Johnson was all but ignored by the alternative media. Although I met with William Greider at *Rolling Stone,* which had done a major piece on Barry Commoner, authored by Lawrence Weschler, now a staff writer with the *New Yorker,* in 1984, *Rolling Stone* never did print an interview with Sonia Johnson.

Adam Hochschild, one of the founders of the Citizens party, was also one of the key editors at *Mother Jones.* This award-winning monthly magazine published out of San Francisco, had done many pieces about Commoner's candidacy in 1980. However, in 1984, *Mother Jones* only did a short interview with Johnson and that was done by one of the interns at the magazine.

Johnson had been the subject of a cover story in *Ms. Magazine* shortly after her book had been published by Doubleday. *Ms.* ran excerpts from the book. However, during the 1984 campaign, *Ms. Magazine* never published an in-depth interview with Sonia Johnson and, in the last stages of the campaign, when one of its journalists did a phone interview with her, Johnson felt the questions were so inane that she had me hand-deliver a letter to Gloria Steinem saying that she did not want the article to run in *Ms.* after the election. However, the issue had already gone to press and the interview ran in the December 1984 edition.

In 1980, Alexander Cockburn wrote many pieces on Barry Commoner in the *Village Voice.* Cockburn, who writes an Op-ed page column for the *Wall Street Journal* every two weeks, never once during the 1984 campaign did an interview with Johnson. This was brought to his attention in a long letter to the editor in the *Nation* magazine. Cockburn responded by dismissing alternative presidential candidates in the 1984 election as a negligible factor.

Lawrence Weschler had written major pieces on Commoner for *Rolling Stone, Los Angeles Weekly,* and the *Los Angeles Times;* however, in 1984, he was a full-time staff writer for the *New Yorker* and at no time did Elizabeth Drew of the *New Yorker* or any of the other journalists at the *New Yorker* ever interview Sonia Johnson.

I also went to the office of Morton Kondracke, who was the editor of the *New Republic* magazine, and who was one of the journalists on the panel during the second nationally televised presidential debate during the 1984 election, but the *New Republic* never interviewed Sonia Johnson.

I went to see the Washington bureau chief of Reuters, the international wire service. *The Economist* had done an in-depth interview with Sonia Johnson and I suggested that Reuters do one; however, the suggestion was declined.

The bottom line, as I see it, having pursued this endeavor for more than four years, is that although other nations in the Western world such as the United Kingdom, Israel and Spain all have multi-party systems, and thus have journalists carefully covering each party, the national news media in the United States again made the decision to cover only the two major political parties.

As Ben Bradlee told me in an interview after the 1980 election, in his opinion, presidential elections in the United States are like a horse race and there's a real "catch 22" involved: If the journalists do not feel you have a chance to win the horse race (meaning if they don't feel you are raising enough money to even qualify, to even be in the horse race) you will receive very little national news media attention and will, therefore, be unable to raise enough money to qualify for the attention from the news media.

# Background on the Citizens Party

The National Citizens Organizing Committee announced its intent to investigate the formation of a new national political party. On December 15, 1979 the Committee filed papers with the Federal Election Commission requesting formal status as the Citizens party.

According to the Citizens party, American voters have learned that whether they vote democratic or republican, the results are the same: large corporations unaccountable to them, increasingly dominate their lives.

Therefore, the message from the American voter is clear: we need a new party in this country — a majority party; a party built on principles, not images; a party which places public interest over private interest; a party whose membership defines and directs party activity, rather than merely casting votes every four years.

The Citizens party held a founding convention in April 1980 in Cleveland to prepare the party platform and nominate candidates for national and local office.

Citizens party organizers included: Ed Barkley, International Association of Machinists and Aerospace Workers; Richard Barnett, author and political scientist; Julian Bond, legislator, state of Georgia; Robert Browne, president, Black Economic Research Center; Adam Hochschild, an editor, *Mother Jones* magazine; Arch Gillies, former head of John Hay Whitney Foundation; Walter Johnson, historian; Maggie Kuhn, Gray Panthers; and Barry Commoner, anti-nuclear activist and author.

Also, Florence McDonald, city councilwoman, Berkeley, California; Don Rose, political consultant; Ed Sadlowski, United Steel Workers of America; Rev. Lucius Walker, director, Interreligious Foundation for Community Organization; Dale Wiehoff, director, U.S. Farmers Association; and Studs Terkel, author.

The Party's Executive Committee was chaired by Jeff Faux, economist, Washington, D.C.

El Partido de la Raza Unida in San Antonio is the official Citizens party representative in Texas, and the Consumer party was the affiliate in Pennsylvania. In California, the Citizens party ran candidates for president and vice-president as independents. This required collecting one hundred thousand valid signatures between mid-June and the end of August, 1980.

The Citizens party was founded August 1979 in Washington, D.C. by a diverse group of progressive leaders, including Commoner, Terkel, Sadlowski, Kuhn, Hochschild, State Senator Bond, Rev. Walker and others.

Citing the complete failure of the Democratic and Republican parties to articulate, let alone confront, the major issues of the day, the Citizens party founders insisted that the time had come for a fundamental realignment of American politics. Although they intended to exert a significant presence in the 1980 presidential elections, their ambition was for the long term and involved the building of a major new political party over the next decade.

The party worked toward its April nominating and platform-writing convention in Cleveland. The party listed its convening principles as the following:

- Public control of energy industries;
- Vigorous support for human rights at home and abroad;
- A swift halt to nuclear power;
- An immediate sharp reversal in the rate of military spending;
- A guaranteed job for everyone who wants to work;
- A strong push for conservation and solar energy;
- Stable prices for the basic necessities of life: food, fuel, housing and medical care;

- Putting the vast corporations which control our economy under OUR control.

In Cleveland, the party refined this program with specific provisions and nominated a 1980 presidential ticket. Barry Commoner, who was a leading spokesperson for the Citizens party, was cited as the likely presidential nominee.

Commoner stated, "It's time we stopped worrying about how to take over the Middle East oil fields and started working to take over the Texas oil fields. We want to introduce a set of issues which we feel will represent historic change in the context of American politics. And we think that 1980 is the year to do it, because the traditional parties have abandoned politics."

In 1980, nationwide, the Citizens party claimed over two thousand members in more than 30 states. California had the largest membership of any state, with Los Angeles membership topping one hundred fifty members after just two meetings and one month of organizing. Citizens party leaders in California organized a petition campaign during the summer of 1980 to secure an independent ballot slot for their candidate in November.

The following is the working paper of the Citizens committee, which was filed with the Federal Election Commission as a political action committee in preparation for organizing a Citizens party. The committee had about one hundred sponsors, including Barry Commoner and Steelworkers Union insurgent Ed Sadlowski.

"One hundred and twenty-five years ago, a small group of people met in a Wisconsin town to form a new political party. They founded the Republican party because neither of the country's major parties were confronting the great national issue of the day: slavery. Today this country is in a similar crisis and faces a similar opportunity. Consider the facts:

Prices have risen more in the past decade than in the 20 years before; and the cost of buying or renting a modest home is soaring beyond the ordinary family's reach. There is no end to inflation in sight.

The wealthiest nation on earth can't provide jobs for its citizens.

Millions are on unemployment or welfare. Among inner city minorities, joblessness is worse than in the Great Depression. College graduates can't find the work for which they have been trained.

Faced with gas lines and a deepening energy crisis, the government compounds the problem. It advocates inflationary decontrol; it dismantled the energy-efficient rail service; it backs expensive and dangerous nuclear power and synthetic fuel; and it largely ignores the major solutions which are clean, decentralized, and potentially cheap energy efficiency and solar power.

The American working man and woman has lost ground. Hard-won raises are erased by inflation. The administration tries to limit wages, but not prices.

A decade and a half after Martin Luther King spelled out his American dream, minorities and the poor are still waiting for their share. The great promises of the 1960's — better housing, job training, national health care, and the rebuilding of our cities — remain a mirage.

After several 'tax reform' bills, there are more loopholes than ever for the rich and the huge corporations; the burden falls still more heavily on the poor and the middle class.

The government already has enough military might to kill everyone on earth. Yet it builds additional new missile systems and weapons to wage electronic war in space. It continues to arm dictatorships around the world; and it pretends that still more billions will buy more security.

Women's gains are under attack. The Equal Rights Amendment is stalled. If she is lucky enough to find a job, the average woman will earn a wage which is 60 percent that of the average man. Small wonder, given all this, that half of the eligible voters don't register, and that half of those who do register usually don't vote. Polls show a plummeting confidence in government and in big business, a pervasive fear that the future will be worse than today. People feel — and rightly — that a dream has been betrayed, that the vision we once allowed ourselves has been replaced by smog-choked skies, by TV screens advertising shoddy products we don't need, and by a country which has somehow, like a car without a driver, slipped from our control.

What happened? Has there been a conspiracy of corporate chieftains or power-hungry politicians to plot a takeover? Of course not. Rather, times have changed. An economic system which in its infancy spread prosperity across a continent, has gradually become outdated.

This country began as a place where people *had* control of their lives, to a degree perhaps unmatched in history; as family farmers, as independent artisans, as entrepreneurs, and as participants in town meeting democracy. The free enterprise economy meant something important: hard work was usually rewarded; if you made as good a product in your workshop as the next person, you prospered; and you did not need a huge capital investment to start a small business.

But our system today no more resembles free enterprise than a freeway resembles a dirt road. Small companies of all kinds are being squeezed out. In many fields — from automobiles to light bulbs to breakfast cereals — four firms or less control more than 90 percent of U.S. production. And more important still, these vast corporations — many with annual budgets greater than those of most countries — spread across national boundaries. A multinational corporation can switch profits to a subsidiary in Panama when we tax it, switch jobs to a plant in Taiwan when American workers ask for higher wages, or make a dangerous pesticide in Brazil when its manufacture is banned in the U.S. For the multinationals, this is no age of 'lowered expectations'; their power is greater than ever. Beholden to no one but stockholders, beyond the control of most governments, these large corporations, which are unaccountable to us, increasingly shape our lives. Their decisions determine what gets produced, and for whom. Auto companies make more money selling high-priced gas-guzzling cars, so they do so — even when the national interest calls for small cars with better mileage, or for trolleys and buses instead. Conglomerates market additive-filled junk food because the profit margin is higher than for fruits and vegetables. Private interests come first, the public interest last. Gradually, almost imperceptibly, a whole lifestyle — energy-intensive, ridden with cancer-causing pollution, fueled by advertising — has been given to us. It is a lifestyle that we did not choose for ourselves.

There is nothing wrong with profit, or with private ownership.

What *is* wrong is when private interest, and not the public good, determines how we live. That is what must be changed, and that is the issue the two major American parties cannot and will not face. Elevating the national interest above vested private interests is the heart of what the Citizens party is about.

What is to be done? We do not have all the solutions. We invite others to join us in enlarging and refining our program. But we believe that, at a bare minimum, a citizens' movement to retake control of this country must work for the following goals:

Public control of the energy industries. In the midst of an energy crisis that affects every American, we cannot let the decisions of Mobil, Exxon and the rest determine how much oil and gas is produced, and where.

If there is not a swift halt to nuclear power, our environment may be poisoned for thousands of years to come. One Three Mile Island accident is enough.

A strong push, instead of the administration's lip service, *for* conservation and solar energy. And for related forms of power such as methane gas and alcohol fuels. These also are safe, non-polluting and can be produced on a small scale by communities across the country, without the multi-billion dollar high-technology plants that only big business can build.

An immediate, sharp reversal in the rate of military spending. Protecting the U.S. from aggression is worthwhile, but building and exporting unneeded new weapons systems has already escalated the arms race to the edge of disaster. A good place to start these cutbacks: the dangerous new MX missile program.

A guaranteed job for everyone who wants to work. National planning and conversion of the armaments industry to productive activity can ensure this.

Stable prices for the basic necessities of life: food, fuel, housing, and medical care. Price controls can accomplish part of that job; more important is to attack inflation's causes — all of which are controllable. One is the massive arms budget, which soaks up hundreds of billions of our dollars but produces nothing people can use. Another is our dependence on the depleting supply of fossil fuel. Whether oil in Saudi Arabia or coal in Kentucky, getting it out of the ground costs more each year than the last.

Vigorous support for human rights at home and abroad. Here, that means working for civil liberties, affirmative action, the ERA, and equal rights to all health care — preventive and therapeutic. Overseas, that means an end to U.S. aid and military alliances with all countries that deny justice to their citizens.

Putting the vast corporations which control our economy under *our* control. We believe in citizen control of major investment and resource decisions. We want to see that control as decentralized as possible. Experiments in worker and community ownership should be encouraged. Cities, town, and neighborhoods should have control over whether a factory with needed jobs can move to another city or country, or whether investors are allowed to abandon an area, leaving it a bombed-out war zone like the South Bronx.

We believe that these are good goals for today — and the future. We are building a Citizens party for the long run. It is not a third party, for we reject the relevance of the two existing ones.

It is a new party, to raise the issues the existing parties ignore. We start today because none of the major party presidential candidates, announced or unannounced, are discussing these issues, and we are tired of wasting our votes.

We ask you to join us. We appeal to republicans and democrats who are fed up with their parties' evasions. We appeal to citizens who have stayed away from the polls and want a party that gives reason to return. We appeal to labor and independent business people, who know that the interests of the giant corporations are not the same as their own. We appeal to the minorities and working people who have suffered the most in the current recession. And we appeal to activists in the women's movement, in the churches, and in the struggle to protect our environment, all of whom have given new meaning to America's democratic traditions in the last few years.

We are embarking on a long but exciting voyage. The economic system we have inherited clearly no longer fits our needs. Such times come in human history. Jefferson knew it when he wrote: "I am not an advocate for frequent changes...but institutions must advance to keep pace with the times. We might as well require a man to wear still the coat which fitted him when a boy, as civilized society to remain ever under the regimen of its ancestors." We have reached the time for one of those historic passages today, and we ask all Americans to join us.

# "Citizens Party Born in Unorthodox Way"

## Special to the New York Times, Cleveland, April 12, 1980
## by
## Warren Weaver, Jr.

With debate echoing long and late through the musty public rooms of a dying hotel, the Citizens party, the latest in an historic series of left-wing progeny, had a difficult and unorthodox birth this weekend.

Some 275 delegates represented 30 states at the founding convention of what they called a second party, rather than a third, on the frequently-stated contention that the republicans and democrats and their prospective candidates were one indistinguishable mass.

Delegates included old radicals of the socialist era, young environmentalists, ardent feminists and labor union activists; almost everyone was an "ist" of some kind. They ranged, for example, from Mario Savio, a Berkeley campus radical of the 1960's to Archibald Gilles, who most recently ran for the New York City Council as a republican.

After hours of procedural dispute and internal politics, the Citizens party today all but nominated Dr. Barry Commoner, the aptly-named ecologist, as its presidential candidate, and LaDonna Harris, a pioneer in native American rights, as his running mate.

Technically, this slate will not be official until ratified by a mail ballot of all party members. However, Harris has no opposition and Dr. Commoner is the sole challenger. Larry Manuel had so little convention support he was forced to nominate himself.

Dr. Commoner, a leading founder of the party last year, had been its assumed presidential candidate from the beginning. Harris, the wife of former-Senator Fred R. Harris, democrat of Oklahoma, became the consensus vice-presidential choice several weeks ago.

Among the goals of the new party are public control of the energy industries, a ban on nuclear power plants, development of solar energy, reduction in military spending, government-guaranteed full employment, price controls to halt inflation and 'citizen control' of major corporate decisions.

Speaker after speaker emphasized how different the Citizens party convention would be from those of the major parties, a goal that was largely realized. Outsiders present could not recall any democratic or republican convention in which the following things took place:

- Major political decisions, like the nomination of national candidates and the adoption of a party platform, were tentative, hinging on final votes by the entire membership after the pressure of the convention had subsided.
- The apparent nominees were not permitted to speak to the convention but were only invited to the rostrum for a silent appearance as delegates applauded.
  "No words, just hugs," declared Harriet Barlow, chairman of the party's executive committee, who was presiding.
- The presidential candidate was not the recipient of the usual rapturous over-wrought praise. Dr. Commoner's nominators, in fact, cited him principally as 'the only person identified with the Citizens party', one who was 'known by a lot of people in the country', and 'a dear old friend of mine'.

The party nominees, Adam Hochschild, publisher of *Mother Jones* magazine indicated, are probably to the right of the membership on many issues and "will not be our leaders in the traditional sense, but our voices."

The environment of the convention was equally unconventional. Recurrent efforts were made from the floor to ban smoking, and one delegate protested that a loud nominating speech had "violated her rights as a human being."

Underlying much of the prolonged debate over convention rules, party constitution and organization, was an obvious division between delegates who were concentrating on promoting the Commoner-Harris ticket in the fall campaign and those who put more emphasis on long-range party building.

Arthur Kinoy of New Jersey summed up the second view when he said, "For the next decade we must build a party from the grass roots to produce the national leadership that can take power in this country."

The Citizens party has already begun a campaign to get its candidates listed on the ballot in as many states as possible. Leaders who believe their ticket can have more than symbolic impact in 1980, lay great stress on the prospect that the major party candidates will be President Carter and Ronald Reagan, more or less equally conservative, and thus unacceptable from the Citizens party point of view.

One Florida delegate quoted Eugene V. Debs, the four-time-losing Socialist candidate for president, as saying, "I would rather vote for what I want and get it."

Keynoting the convention last night, Studs Terkel, the Chicago writer, predicted that the new party would "reclaim the American dream from the predators who've stolen it — that's what this meeting is all about." He said Cleveland was "so poetically right" for the first convention because it had become famous for populist mayors.

The Cleveland Plaza hotel, where the convention was held, closed its doors at the end of the month to be gutted for conversion into an office building.

Since the Party was formally recognized last week as a national political organization by the Federal Election Commission, it can

As a result of this government/corporate collaboration, corporations have achieved tax and other subsidies, access to venture capital, rollbacks of consumer and environmental restraints on corporate operations and loopholes in the anti-trust laws. These achievements work to increase unemployment and inflation, decrease productivity and promote the continued inappropriate use of resources. Meanwhile, they contribute to corporate profitability which is dependent on:

- a sufficient level of unemployment to maintain an inexpensive and mobile labor force;
- minimal competition in the marketplace in order to maintain high prices which provide a higher margin of profit;
- production that yields the highest profit rather than production of necessities such as mass transit systems and low middle-income housing.

Corporate power extends to the American family farm which is increasingly dominated by vertically-integrated and tightly-concentrated agribusiness corporations. For rural America, this control of our food economy means soaring farm production costs; unfair and widely fluctuating prices for agricultural products; credit available only at exorbitant rates; and oppressive market power wielded by a small, select circle of competing interests.

In addition to the problem of corporate power, a second source of America's economic ills is the extremely large military budget. Resources are drained from productive uses (e.g., modernizing the steel mills—developing solar technology/education) whenever government spending goes to building fighter planes, bombs and high-tech weaponry. Defense spending aggravates unemployment because it creates far fewer jobs than other forms of government spending. Inflation, too, is aggravated as the products of military spending are not put to any constructive use.

Thus, the more money put into military spending, the weaker the economy. Indeed, it has been shown that, for the period of 1960-1979, the leading industrialized countries show a close, inverse relationship between the size of their military budget and their economic performance. And the United States is at the bottom of the list with an average productivity growth of less than three percent per year and average military expenditures of nearly seven percent of the GNP. The Citizens party calls for building a new economy, one in which workers and consumers exercise democratic control over the economic decisions that separate the promise of American society from its reality. This task requires a direct challenge to established corporate and privileged interests.

The issue here is economic democracy. The people must have a voice in deciding such essential questions as: What goods and services shall be produced; what prices shall be charged and toward what ends the wealth of the nation shall be invested. To achieve this democracy, the Citizens party supports small businesses and family farms, producer and consumer cooperatives, community-based and community-owned firms, and worker self-management as well as worker ownership of plants.

We must reassert effective public control over national energy resources development, production, marketing mechanisms and pricing — all of which are now dominated by private corporations. We must move toward a decentralized system of renewable energy sources which will strengthen the economy at its base.

## II.  Citizens Party Economic Policy

Beneath the overriding theme of economic democracy, the Citizens party economic policy focuses on six areas: public governance, achieving full employment, environment and resources, investment policy, halting inflation and reforming the tax structure.

### A.  Public Governance
1.  The Citizens party proposes to place irresponsible corporations under public control. Public control means effective and strict regulation as well as initiatives toward a more democratic economy.

2.  Regulations would include:
  • a requirement that boards of directors be representative of workers and consumers;

- requiring certain conglomerates (particularly energy producers) to divest themselves horizontally of their holdings in other industries; and vertically of distribution systems, shipping facilities and retail sales outlets;
- stricter tax laws (see below).
- price controls (see below).

Initiatives for economic democracy would include tax breaks and programs for:
- worker ownership and self management;
- community-based and community-owned firms;
- producer and consumer cooperatives;
- small business and family farms.

The economic transformation envisioned by the Citizens party will involve a major shift in the relations between workers and their places of employment, which will affect the role of organized labor. Labor unions in America have won considerable rights and benefits for the American people, but with a persistent downward trend in the economy, these gains are being eroded. In addition, the unions have often become centralized, autocratic organizations. We support Labor in the effort to democratize organizations and gain control over both their own working conditions and the policy decision of the corporations. We believe that a safe and satisfying job, quality products, efficient production, and control over one's life go hand in hand. We support extending the benefits of union organization to the entire work force and the elimination of all laws that deter collective bargaining.

3. We support the creation of publicly-owned and operated business in a few instances, e.g., utilities, railroads, and mass transit. In other industries, if regulations or initiatives for public control are inadequate, public ownership should be instituted. Public ownership should be implemented at the last centralized level feasible and in such a way as to make the industry more accountable to the public.

B.  Full Employment

The Citizens party supported a program providing a job or job training to every American wanting to work. Public employment in such areas as housing, health, environment, mass transit, and education would alleviate drastic shortages which the private market has failed to fill. Specific priorities would be set by local community boards who could decide how best to use the government funded jobs to fulfill local plans. Compared with the costs of unemployment (in terms of welfare rolls, crime, unemployment compensation, and decreased tax revenues), the full employment program would be cost effective; the production and spending power of the employed would bring revenue to the government.

Street crime, which is inextricably linked to social and economic problems (especially unemployment), will be greatly reduced by the full employment program. The cost of street crime, both social and economic (in terms of the crime victims who experience mental, physical or material harm, and the criminals, who are sent to prisons supported by tax dollars), will be greatly reduced as well.

C.  Inflation

Obviously, the public governance and full employment will be partial solutions to the problem of inflation. In the interest of ending inflation, the Citizens party proposes initially to place price controls on the basic necessities: food, housing, medical care and a minimal level of energy. But price controls are not, in themselves, an adequate long-range solution to the problem of inflation. If the program merely acts to subsidize low-income or other consumers, this will increase demand without encouraging a parallel increase in supply, resulting in pressure to raise prices. For price controls to work responsibly, there must be concurrent encouragement to increase supply.

In the energy industry, such encouragement will be ineffective so long as we are dependent on nonrenewable sources of energy. As a nonrenewable energy source is depleted, it becomes progressively more costly to produce. Each additional increment of oil, coal or gas is harder to find and harder and harder to extract from the ground; thus, continued reliance on these sources means an unending escalation in prices. No economic system can withstand the pressures of unending escalation in prices. No economic system can withstand the pressures of unending inflation. Since nonrenewable energy promises such a future, sooner or later it must be replaced by renewable energy — which is stable in cost. The Citizens party proposes such a transition using the variety of solar energy forms: wood, biomass, photovoltaic, low-head hydro, wind turbine, and co-generation.

In the areas of housing, while rent control by itself can never be a solution to a community's long-term housing problems, it may be appropriate as a holding action while other policies (such as the use of public employment to build low-middle income housing) are developed and implemented.

In the oil, steel, auto, rubber and cereal industries, three or four companies have, for years, colluded to administer prices in those industries in blatant violation of anti-trust laws. Through the anti-corporate policies discussed above, the Citizens party would put an end to this inflationary and monopolistic practice.

Expenditures of vast sums of money on uneconomic military programs have been another major cause of inflation. The Citizens party proposes conversion of the American weapons industry to socially useful production.

D.   Environment and Resources:

Building productivity at the expense of environmental quality, public health and conservation of natural resources is a cruel fraud that benefits only the current corporate elite, and even them only for a short time. Environmental protection is in fact an inseparable part of economic prosperity, and environmental quality, the undeniable birthright of all living things.

E.   Investment Policy:

Control over investment determines the health, direction and equity of the economy. The U.S. economy has been pirated for years by bank, corporate, and governmental policies that have emphasized short-term profit at the expense of innovation and long-term economic health, the few at the expense of the many, private accumulation at the expense of public works — and the present at the expense of the future.

Reinvestment, reindustrialization and reorientation of the economy are essential, and must proceed through democratic planning at the local, regional and national scale. Specifically, the Citizens party proposes that:

- Democratically controlled municipal, state, county and federal financial institutions be created to channel and foster investment in socially productive enterprises;
- Economic democracy be furthered by establishing community and work-place planning groups to guide the use of the tax system and the allocation of capital retained by public financial institutions;
- Union pension funds be controlled democratically by unions;
- Any public assistance to the private business sector be strictly conditional on full cooperation with meeting public goals of sustainability and social justice.

F.  Tax Reform

In recent years, the American system of taxation has increasingly shifted the burden of taxes onto those less able to pay while corporations and the wealthy have taken advantage of tax abatements, loopholes, shelters and subsidies. The Citizens party proposes to restructure the American system of taxation to make it fair, comprehensive, simple and accountable.

Specifically, the Citizens party proposes the following tax reforms:

- A sharply progressive tax on individuals and corporations with large amounts of income, wealth or profits;
- An end to tax abatements, loopholes, and subsidies to large corporations;
- Tax incentives to worker-owned firms and community cooperatives.

Foreign and Military Policy
III. International Policies for Peace, Justice and Environmental
    Survival.

For the last generation, we have lived in a world of opposing
power blocs and of corporate entanglement in other countries. This
has almost led to nuclear war (most notably in Democratic President
Kennedy's 'Cuban Missile Crisis') and has led to large-scale American
intervention in the Dominican Republic and Vietnam.

Recent world economic difficulties heighten the risk of war; these
difficulties are rooted in economic systems that put the need for
economic and military competitiveness ahead of the needs and
wishes of the people. Economic difficulties made the people of the
United States more receptive to proposals to make war upon Iran in
1980. Economic failure in Argentina and Britain led tottering regimes
to use military adventures in the Malvinas/Falkland Island to regain
popular support. Economic difficulties lead corporations to squeeze
workers harder, lead landed aristocracies in the third world to
squeeze the peasantry harder; and the resulting social unrest leads
to threats of intervention by the U.S. or other powers whose corporations feel threatened by popular democratic rebellion. Economic
hard times lead companies to push government for enlarged arms
expenditures — which creates an escalating arms race. And the social,
economic and political effects of these insurgencies and the arms race
spill over both to worsen the economic crisis by wasting investment
capital, materials and human labor, and to increase fear of invasion
among countries neighboring those most directly involved.

Thus, hard times become dangerous times. At the moment, wars
rage in the South Atlantic, Afghanistan and the Persian Gulf. Enmity
between Russia and the U.S. has increased; and strains have widened
within the power blocs as conflicting interests tear at existing
economic and political interests among Japan, Western Europe and
the United States; within Western Europe itself and within the
Warsaw Pact.

Atomic war is a real possibility, as is the risk of American
involvement in lesser wars. The question is: What can we do? To the
extent that the pressures toward war stem from political and

economic decision-making by corporate elites or state bureaucracies that are independent of popular democratic control, movements such as our own can weaken the forces that push toward war. By democratizing control over the government and wresting it from the hands of corporations with investments abroad and arms contracts at home, we put the power over war and peace in the hands of those who suffer from war rather than those who gain by it.

Human survival is also threatened by environmental catastrophe. Narrowing economic decision by corporations and state bureaucracies around the world cause increasingly dangerous pollution of our air, water and food supplies by chemical, industrial and nuclear wastes. Only popular control of all economic decisions can preserve ecological survival.

A movement for popular control that is isolated in the United States cannot solve these problems. Our economic difficulties are international as well as national; the threat of war comes from conflicting interests between ruling elites and from the behavior of transnational corporations. Ecological catastrophe likewise requires worldwide action. Thus, our peace and survival depend upon democratizing control over the economy and governments in all countries. We apply support and depend upon environmental activists such as those in the Green parties; the peace movements in Western Europe, Japan and Eastern Europe; and the popular movements against dictatorship and foreign domination in El Salvador, Poland and elsewhere.

In contrast, consider the foreign policy of the democrats and republicans. They sponsor increased armaments, and support autocratic regimes in Central America, Chile, and white minority rule in South Africa. This risks more Vietnams and it recklessly invites atomic war. Under the doctrine of "flexible response", some corporate-minded politicians and military officers perfect ways to intervene against movements like our own in other countries. Both Carter and Reagan have sought a first strike capability — a madness which pretends that nuclear war could be "winnable". Instead, such policies increase the danger of total annihilation.

The Citizens party believes that there is a better path to peace than the patronage of war. The United States' war-like foreign policy should be replaced with a policy that undertakes, quite literally, acts of friendship. A genuine peace will enable the vast physical, financial, and human resources now wasted in the illusory attempt to gain national security through military strength to be used productively.

We must develop a foreign policy which clearly distinguishes between the interests and security of the American people and those of private corporations. The Citizens party pledges to commit U.S. foreign and military policy to the principles of non-intervention in the internal affairs of other countries, and the inviolability of the right of all people to self-determination.

The Citizens party supports an end to compulsory military registration and draft of young people.

Human and Equal Rights
IV. Citizens Party Analysis and Position

Throughout American history, our society has treated women, minorities, the elderly, children, homosexuals and the disabled unjustly. In recent years, we have accomplished some fundamental progress toward providing a more free and just culture. However, the economic and social barriers to achieving equality remain:

- The rights and gains made by black Americans over the last quarter century have not produced economic and political equality for blacks;
- Most elderly Americans are healthy and yet they are all too often institutionalized, preventing them from participation in independent life;
- This country is still controlled by a patriarchy which oppresses women socially as well as economically;
- Discrimination in housing, education, jobs and health care still occurs too often.

As a result of corporate power the government has failed to oppose big business, whose control of the economy keeps women, minorities and the elderly in their disadvantaged positions. These groups, which are the majority of the poor population, are the hardest hit by unemployment and inflation which the government has left unchecked.

Of additional concern is the threat of the New Right movement. The attack on affirmative action, the attempt to repeal the Voting Rights Act and other civil rights legislation, the attacks on women's rights such as ERA, reproductive rights and Title IX, the continued disregard for the elderly and the poor on fixed incomes, the rollback in school busing plans and the new uncontrolled rise of racist sentiment, are all the opening stages of the New Right's attempt to counter recent human rights victories.

To insure the treatment of each individual as an equal and integral member of a just and healthy society, the Citizens party promotes and seeks to create a strong and open non-sexist and non-racist society in which all people will be free to develop to their full potential. The Citizens party opposes the use of sex, class, race or sexual orientation as obstacles to the enjoyment of a decent income, good housing, quality education and medical care.

It is a priority of the Citizens party to seek to improve the status of women in our society. Women must have the right to choose in every aspect of their lives. Most fundamentally, reproductive freedoms must be secured. On a broader level, women must have the same options as men in employment, education, health care and family life. But the problem of sexism is not purely a legal or economic one. The Citizens party therefore seeks, through education and political action, to overcome sexism and end the male domination which limits women's freedoms.

Citizens Party Policies on Human and Equal Rights
V. A. Employment Rights

The Citizens party program of full employment (see Economy section of this document) would assure jobs for everyone willing and able to work, with special programs for minorities and youth. This would be the first step toward redistributing the wealth which is currently concentrated in the hands of the white male population.

The Citizens party opposes employment discrimination on the basis of sex, race, age, sexual preference, disability or ethnic background. Specifically, the Citizens party supports:

- Equal Pay for work of comparable value;
- The implementation of programs such as flexible work-times and work-place child-care;
- Full implementation of affirmative action programs;
- The right of the elderly and the disabled to jobs and job training;
- Improved work and safety standards. Regulations and compensation for job-related injury;
- Increased penalties for health-safety violations;
- The protection of migrant workers against unjust and exploitative treatment.

B.   Education Rights:

The Citizens party pledges to support a public education system which provides opportunity for children of all classes and social conditions; encourages personal development; and nurtures an understanding of human rights, responsibilities and freedoms. We are committed to challenging racism as it is manifested within the educational system. We support desegregation and efforts to expand multi-cultural and bilingual education. Adequate educational programs for the physically, mentally or emotionally disabled must be provided to insure their full participation in society.

C.   Health Care Rights

A health care system based on private ownership of facilities and fees determined by profit margins cannot and will not provide adequate service equally to all members of our society. We recognize the need for redress in the distribution of our national health resources. Priority must be given to those people — the poor, the elderly, the disabled, racial minorities, women and those living in rural and central city areas — who have traditionally been deprived of adequate health services. Specific human rights related to health care policies include:

- Safe, effective, low cost contraception and abortion (including federal funding for abortion) must be available;
- Health care programs to compensate for illness which is the result of government or corporate abuse of citizens (e.g., residents of Love Canal, Vietnam Vets subjected to agent orange, victims of black or brown lung);
- Seating elderly citizens on boards of health care agencies that affect their lives;
- Pregnancy, maternity and paternity benefits on the job;
- Development of a comprehensive national health service emphasizing preventive health care measures.

D.  Right to Non-Violence

We reject the acceptance of violence as normal in family and social relationships. Measures to stem increasing racial violence must be enacted. We support programs which provide strong, effective measures to combat rape, including rape within marriage; active reform of existing rape laws; and legal and medical support for rape victims. We affirm the right of children to be free from emotional, physical and sexual abuse by their parents, relatives or other adults. We must provide shelters for battered women and children as well as legal resources and counseling for victims and their families.

E.  Housing rights

The Citizens party opposes discrimination in housing and the redlining practices of bankers and insurance companies which devalue and segregate minority communities. We also support legislation to prevent the forced displacement of existing residents as a result of gentrification.

F.  The Rights of Puerto Rico, the District of Columbia, and Native Americans

The Citizens party supports the rights of the people of the District of Columbia to statehood; the rights of the people of Puerto Rico to statehood or independence, whichever they choose; and the rights of native American people to have full control over their lands. We

39

call for the government to honor its treaty agreements with native American peoples and an end to public and private exploitation of native American lands.

G.   Freedom of Sexual Preference

The ultimate invasion of the dignity of human beings by government is the intrusion into their private sexual lives. We support the repeal of all laws covering private sexual conduct between consenting adults. Discrimination based on sexual orientation or marital status in child custody, adoption and inheritance cases should be ended.

# An Interview with Barry Commoner

Rolling Stone, *May 1, 1980, p. 44-48*
*by*
*Lawrence Weschler*

"I don't know about you," Barry Commoner was telling an enthusiastic audience of eight hundred in Los Angeles a month ago, "but I'm tired of having to hold my nose every time I enter my polling booth, and I think it's time we did something about it." From the sound of it, the crowd concurred. They had gathered on ten days notice despite a pelting rain. They looked wet. They did not look radical. Indeed, if Commoner was talking revolution, his audience looked anything but revolutionary. To be sure, there were the usual stalwarts, the tired veterans of the sixties, but there were also senior citizens, blue-collar workers, housewives, teen-agers and small businessmen. "Where are all these people coming from?" marveled one smiling activist. "I've been organizing rallies around here for 15 years and I've never seen most of these faces." They had come from all over to cheer Commoner's assertion that, with the democrats and republicans rushing headlong to abandon political issues, it is time to form a new party.

So in August of last year, Commoner joined almost one hundred other progressive activists (including author Studs Terkel; dissident United Steelworkers leader Ed Sadlowski; *Mother Jones*' publisher, Adam Hochschild; Gray Panther leader Maggie Kuhn and Georgia State Legislator, Julian Bond) in launching the Citizens party. That

41

party is still in the process of defining itself, but it already claims chapters in more than 30 states. While gearing up for its ultimate goal of building a majoritarian party over the next 15 years, the Citizens party also seems intent on offering a substantial presence in the 1980 presidential elections. At press time, most observers were predicting that following its convention in Cleveland from April 11th through 13th, the Citizens party's principal spokesperson would also be its presidential nominee.

Barry Commoner first came into prominence in the late fifties for his fight against above ground nuclear weapons testing. During the late sixties and into the seventies, Commoner was at the forefront of the environmental movement. In 1970, *Time* featured him on its cover, dubbing him "The Paul Revere of Ecology." His work is grounded in the laboratory but his focus is the world, and for years he has supplemented his work with appearances at anti-nuke rallies, colleges, union meetings and farmers' conventions. Commoner's abiding conviction is that scientists have a responsibility to make their work tangibly public.

Born in Brooklyn in 1917, he received his bachelor's degree in zoology from Columbia in 1937 and his doctorate in biology from Harvard in 1941. He has been a professor of biology at St. Louis' Washington University since 1947, and since 1965 the director of its prestigious Center for the Biology of Natural Systems, one of the world's leading think tanks on environmental and economic issues. His best selling books include *Science and Survival* (1966), *The Closing Circle* (1971), *The Poverty of Power* (1976) and *The Politics of Energy* (1979) originally serialized last spring in the *New Yorker.*

During the past decade, Commoner's perspective has become increasingly political. It's not so much that he's left his academic field in quest of politics — politics, rather, have invaded his domain with a vengeance. For, as he says, it's no longer merely a matter of academic contention which industrial methods are the most energy efficient, and which economic alternatives the most ecologically sound. On such issues rests the fate of this nation as it enters the eighties.

For the past several months, Commoner and other party luminaries have been on a national tour for the Citizens party. For his two days in Los Angeles, his sidekick is Studs Terkel, the scrappy, endearing chronicler of the lives of American working people in such books as *Working* and *Hard Times.* "I want," he tells the delighted crowd, "to be for Barry Commoner what Frank Sinatra is for Ronald Reagan." A few minutes later everyone comes surging to their feet when Commoner insists "The time has come to move beyond protest and to begin the work of taking power."

It's a long-term goal, and some would say a desperate long shot. But many political activists see few immediate options in the miserable debacle of election year 1980. And they're willing to give the long-term strategy a try. The fundraiser in Los Angeles at the home of Gore Vidal, proved a success both politically and financially. The next morning, at his hotel, Commoner slowed down for a few hours, and we had this conversation.

Q.     There's a lot of confusion these days on a relatively straight-forward point: Are we or are we not running out of oil?

A.     President Carter came down from his solitude on Camp David and claimed that we were. Basically, he was being as truthful as Abraham Lincoln would have been, had he made the same point in 1860. The reason is that in 1859 we drilled our first oil well, and we've been running out of oil ever since. So what Carter said was correct but, shall we say, irrelevant. The important fact is that with a nonrenewable resource — oil, coal, uranium and so forth — the cost will go up along an exponential curve — that is, it will rise rather slowly for a long time and then suddenly arch upward at an ever-increasing rate. That's the key to the entire energy situation and, indeed, to much of our economic crisis.

Q.     Why does the cost of a nonrenewable resource go up at an exponential rate?

A.     There are various ways to explain it. Let's say I give you a bowl of spaghetti and tell you there will be no seconds. There. You've got yourself a nonrenewable resource. Now, let's work out the cost in terms of the energy required to get the spaghetti out of the bowl and into your mouth. It turns out that the first several forksful are easy, but as you get to the bottom of the bowl, it gets tougher, and after a while you're using an awful lot of energy, scrabbling around for those last few forksful. That's exactly what happens with oil. The fact is, we will never run out of oil; at some point, it will simply require more energy to extract a barrel of oil than is contained in that barrel, and hopefully, when that happens, we will have the wisdom not to go after it.

In the meantime, we've got a serious problem, because the purpose of energy is to run everything in the economy. But the energy system has begun cannibalizing the economic system it is supposed to fuel. It has caused our double-digit inflation, because if you are spending more and more of the output just to keep the machinery running, there is less left for consumption, and prices go up.

Q.     What realistic options do we have?

A.     Obviously one way or another we have to get onto renewable resources, where the cost will be level over time. There are basically three: fusion, nuclear with a breeder reactor and solar. Let me quickly dismiss fusion for a very simple reason — it doesn't exist. They are doing experiments, and bless them, maybe it will work. Maybe they will be able to contain the radioactivity or the temperatures which run into the millions of degrees. But not even its greatest proponents expect any fusion for at least 25 years. By that time, we will have been driven to the wall by the rising cost of energy. The crisis is now.

Q.     What about nuclear?

A.     The present nuclear power system is not renewable. If operated on the scale that has been projected, we will run out of uranium in 25 to 30 years. And of course, across that period, the price of uranium will also trace an exponential curve. The only way to get renewable energy out of uranium is through a breeder reactor which generates additional fuel as it generates electricity. But controlling such reactors is very tricky. They're much harder to control than the kind of system at Three Mile Island. When nuclear power was first introduced, they kept promising us how it was going to be 'too cheap to meter'. Well, that just hasn't proved to be the case, and indeed, there were no new commissions in 1979 and only two in 1978, with so many strings attached that in effect there were none then, either. And that was before the accident at Three Mile Island, in the aftermath of which costs are only going to increase that much more.

Think about it: a fundamental principle of thermodynamics is that it's a good idea to match the source of energy to the character of the task. For example, a work-requiring task is warming a baby's bottle. It won't happen by itself. So you put the bottle in a pot of warm water, and that is an appropriate way to warm the baby's milk. There are other ways; you could use a blowtorch. But the intensity of the energy is beyond what is required. It is an inherently dangerous way to warm a milk bottle. You'll break the bottle, spill the milk, cut your hand — or you'll have to invest a small fortune on devices to safeguard against these eventualities.

Now, what's the work-requiring task in a nuclear plant? It's simple: to boil water, to make steam, to turn the turbines, to produce electricity. The hard part is, what are they using to boil the water? They're using radiation, and that's simply an inappropriate way to boil water. How do we know that? The entire history of the nuclear industry proves it.

The Three Mile Island Kemeny Commission put its finger on the problem when they said, 'Nuclear power is inherently dangerous'. It is dangerous in a way that has to be actively protected against; and that protection — in the form of prior studies, construction safeguards, backup systems and shutdown time — dramatically effects the cost.

Q.    Aren't we so reliant on nuclear power that we just can't shut down the reactors?

A.    That's a myth, one which Carter has been promulgating, and for a while he was joined in it by Kennedy. We could shut down three-fourths of the nuclear power plants around the country and all of them around Chicago — the statistic they both cite — without any loss of electricity. That's because non-nuclear plants — coal-burners, for example — are operating at a very low capacity, only 37 to 40 percent in the Chicago area.

Q.    Wouldn't such a transfer result in increased pollution and perhaps increased cost?

A.     Yes, it would. We calculated a 10 percent increase in pollution and five percent in cost. The point is that there is a choice, and isn't that a choice the people ought to be given? Carter and Kennedy would have us believe there's no choice; we have to have nuclear. The issue is not which is the right thing to do, but rather, what is it in the system that is preventing us from discussing the choice?

Q.     What is your prognosis for the antinuclear movement?

A.     In two or three years, we will see the end of nuclear power in the United States. The nuclear divisions of companies like General Electric and Westinghouse, for example, are so economically troubled they will have to go before Congress for a Chrysler-style bail out, and at that point, we will at long last have a national debate on whether we want nuclear power. I believe that those who oppose its further development will win the battle.

You're already beginning to see the contours of the industry's position. They'll try to tie the need for nuclear power into the potential shortfalls of Arab oil — which, of course, misses the point that nuclear energy cannot be converted economically into liquid fuel to power cars. That's what the oil crisis is all about. Furthermore, they'll make a big pitch along national security lines, which is even more preposterous. Nuclear power stations are terribly susceptible to sabotage or catastrophic accident; their by-products can be stolen and turned into weapons, and in the event of war, nothing could present a more dangerous target.

Incidentally, when I'm on college campuses or at anti-nuke rallies and I make that assertion about the end of nuclear power, people get all excited. But I have to tell them to wait, calm down, because that's only a beginning. What, I ask them is the moral responsibility of the victor? I mean, I'm a veteran of the anti-war movement. We stopped an immoral war, and in the process, deposed two presidents. In any sensible political system, a movement *that* successful would be in power today. Instead, where are we? We won, and then everybody went home. The question we must address this time is how we can turn a successful protest movement into political power.

Q.   Which brings us to the subject of solar energy.

A.   Often, when you bring up solar energy, people scoff and say, 'Oh well, that's for the year 2000'. The first point to be made is that all the major solar technologies are already feasible, and they are economically competitive or could be very shortly; the only thing that stands in the way of a solar transition is politics.

Certain inappropriate deployments of solar energy would prove exorbitantly expensive, principally those that rely on the same kinds of concentrated networks used by our coal and nuclear-based systems. Keep in mind that when we speak of solar energy, we're not just speaking of the sun's light and heat. We are also talking about such solar-derived energy sources as wind and hydro/electric conversion, alcohol production and methane harvesting. Most of these technologies need to be instituted in a decentralized manner, because the sun provides a diffuse source of energy. And that decentralization, as much as anything, accounts for the intense opposition from centralized corporations and government agencies. A centralized energy network gives those people power, decentralization threatens that power. Still, solar energy is no moral panacea, even if it's decentralized. There are ways of introducing solar energy that will exacerbate the impact of the energy crisis on the poor.

Q.   Can you give an example?

A.   Well, California pioneered one way with the 55 percent tax credit on installing solar devices. That sounds good, but think about it; who benefits and who pays? Most of the cost of solar energy is the front-end capital investment, which can be paid off at a fixed rate. Okay, under the California system, people who can't afford to borrow $20,000 to buy a solar heating system for their homes, say, because they're poor or because they're renters — what are renters going to do — take the device with them when they move? These people are really excluded from achieving that kind of solar input; and solar energy becomes available only to the relatively wealthy people.

The poor and the lower-middle class end up paying much of the rich people's solar conversion costs. We've just found out that about three-fourths of the California tax credits have been for solar heaters for swimming pools. So social welfare programs get cut, because state revenues go down. And then, as more and more individual homes cut themselves off from the established utilities, the utilities raise their prices on everyone who can't afford to buy a solar unit. That's just clearly the wrong way to go about it.

Q.      What would be the right way?

A.      Just think of an urban situation such as the kind you find in the south Bronx or the part of Brooklyn where I grew up. Those areas need to be rebuilt, the housing is standing, but the heating systems have to be replaced. Well, I would put in a neighborhood power plant — servicing, let's say, 10 square blocks — run as a cogenerator. That's a generator that produces electricity and also recaptures up to two-thirds of the heat that's ordinarily thrown off as waste. That heat is then distributed through a district heating system. In other words, you wouldn't have a separate furnace at each house, you'd have all that warm water circulating in underground pipes around the neighborhood.

Now solar collectors could be installed in the neighborhood system wherever they made sense so that even if you were a renter or lived in a house shaded by trees, you could still benefit. Likewise, as those solar panels, which are made of photovoltaic cells, become economically competitive, they could be installed above parking lots or schools, and their contribution could be similarly pooled.

Also, since you have a neighborhood power station, the only feasible fuel would be natural gas, because it burns cleanly; any other fuel would be so polluting no one would want to live by the plant,and that would open up a third solar application. The City's sewage could be converted into solar methane at local plants, and the methane could be used to replace a good deal of the natural gas. Kelp in coastal regions or cattails in Minnesota could supplement methane generation, or wind-powered generators could supplement electrical needs. Each neighborhood would be different.

The main point, though, is that the only way to avoid a solar transition that benefits only the rich is to embark upon it as a collective enterprise, an integration of resources.

Q.     A moment ago, you claimed that all solar technologies are currently economically feasible. Yet a panel of photovoltaic (PV) cells now runs about 10 dollars a watt, which means something like one thousand dollars to run a 100-watt bulb.

A.     That's true, because the PV industry today is roughly in the same position that the integrated circuitry industry was, say, 15 years ago — you know, those tiny chips that allow for pocket calculators. Most of the technology behind those chips existed then, but they were terribly expensive. It would probably have cost several hundred dollars for a pocket calculator. Turns out the military needed microcomputers for missiles, satellites and so forth. They put in such huge orders that over a period of six years, the industry was able to put in mass assembly operations and the price dropped from 50 dollars per chip to two dollars and fifty cents. At that price, the chips suddenly flooded the commercial market in all the applications we know about: watches, calculators, etc.

Well, the Federal Energy Administration (FEA) was asked by Congress a few years back to study the feasibility of helping PV cells to become economically competitive. So these fellows asked the Department of Defense how large an order they'd be interested in making — that is, in instances where solar is already cost-competitive or cheaper than the sources they were using. The department told the FEA they could use one hundred fifty million watts of PV cells. So the FEA then checked with the industry and said, 'Look, if we gave you an order for that many watts of PV cells, what would you charge us?' The answer came back something like this: They're now 10 dollars a watt. In the first year they'd go down to three dollars a watt, and by the fifth year, to fifty cents a watt. Now, at three dollars a watt, PV cells become more economical for use in distant irrigation pumping stations than the current gasoline-powered devices. Also, the UN offered to buy millions of dollars' worth at that price, because it's a better way for an underdeveloped country to set up an electrical system than building central power stations. At one dollar a watt, they would be economical for street lighting. And at fifty cents, they would be economical for residential lighting.

All that would have been required was an initial government investment of four hundred forty million — indeed, by not spending that money, the government was wasting funds on more expensive electrical generation devices. In fact, Congress did tack on a substantial allocation for PV cells in the National Energy Act, which was eventually passed. But when Carter signed that bill, he refused to authorize that particular expenditure. Whereupon Solarex, one of the main manufacturers, proposed a joint venture with Montedison to build the world's largest PV plant outside Florence, Italy. Oh, don't worry, within a few years we'll have them. But they'll be made in Italy and Japan, and by buying them we'll increase our balance-of-payments problem.

Q.     What about the need for car fuel, which seems to be, after all, the most immediate problem?

A.     This brings us to the subject of gasohol — a blend of ninety percent gasoline and ten percent alcohol — the kind that could be readily distilled in solar fashion from Midwestern corn. That alcohol is a superb octane booster. It turns out that the main reason for the gas lines is that the oil companies failed to build refineries that could produce the high-octane boosters necessary for lead-free gasoline. I'll put it to you very simply: If we had had the wit two years ago to ask Chrysler to mass produce Model-T alcohol stills and loan them out to farms, there would have been no gas lines last summer. Why isn't it being done? Farmers all over the Midwest are ready to do it; some are even starting to put money into stills — but they're worried. They don't know whether the oil companies will cooperate. After awhile, if they want to put in more that ten percent alcohol, car engines will have to be modified. So farmers have a funny problem, which is not quite amenable to the free market; they have to worry about integrating with two other industries before they can begin.

Q.     But isn't a massive gasohol program part of Carter's package to get rid of the glut occasioned by the Soviet grain embargo?

A.    At the time Carter made that proposal, our center did some preliminary analyses, which indicated that introducing a gasohol program in this hasty, ill-considered fashion would prove impossible or disastrous or both.

A program like this has to be thought out. You're asking farmers to make a substantial investment in distilling equipment, an investment they'll handsomely recoup over the years, but not because of a one-shot grain surplus. The best way to distill and collect alcohol is through decentralized, small-scale operations. One of the biggest boondoggles looms because Carter seems to think that if you turn five million dollars worth of corn into alcohol, you've thereby taken all that grain off the market. On the contrary, the thing that makes gasohol so commercially attractive to farmers is that the by-product of the distilling process is high-quality cattle feed. So sure, right now, you take all that corn off the market, six months from now the market for soybeans — another source of cattle feed — may be totally disrupted.

Q.    Awhile back, the energy situation seemed to be the foremost concern on the American political scene. In recent months, however, Iran and Afghanistan have occupied center stage, and with that, some feel, has come a pronounced lurch to the right among American voters.

A.    I don't see that, necessarily. First of all, you have to realize that Iran and the energy situation are two aspects of the same crisis. The principal reason Southwest Asia has become such a focus of anxious concern is because of the oil there. The only real solution to the problem is for us to become self-reliant, as quickly as possible, and the only way to do that is through a solar transition.

There's no question but that the longer we wait in embarking on that transition, the greater the risk of war. Secretary of Defense Harold Brown returned from the Middle East last year and announced that we were going to create a large mobile force prepared for speedy deployment into that area — and that was before Iran and Afghanistan. Let me make one point: no military action will insure the supply of oil. I think that if we want to insure a supply of oil — and make sure that the people in control really produce the oil — it's the Texas oil fields we should be taking over, not the Middle East oil fields.

Q.  If the solar transition makes as much sense as you claim, and given the growing risk of war, why isn't the choice self-evident? Why aren't we going solar? Why is the federal government paralyzed?

A.  It's not only paralyzed, it's anarchy. You have to remember that Carter came into office proclaiming that the single issue on which his administration was to be judged was its success in framing a comprehensive energy policy. Well, he's failed. And he's failed after having made several contradictory attempts. He began with a national energy plan, which was introduced under the guise of being conservation-based when it was in fact heavily steeped in nuclear and coal. After confusing everyone with this misleading presentation, he was only able to get Congress to decontrol the price of natural gas. And we've seen the terrible impact that's had on inflation. Then he went into that solitude at Camp David and came down with basically Nelson Rockefeller's plan of several years earlier, which was to take one hundred billion dollars in federal funds and hand them over to private industry so companies could develop synthetic fuels. That is another nonrenewable resource with a guaranteed exponential cost factor and a resource that wouldn't come on line for at least 15 or 20 years, not to mention all the carcinogenic side effects.

I don't see how we can continue to deal with people who go on formulating and passing bills like that. This government has proved itself incapable of confronting the energy issues. I'm not calling for a protest movement. There's nothing to protest. At some point, the people will have to rise up and insist that there actually be, for the first time, a national energy policy.

The bottom line is this: The decisions about what we produce, how we produce it, what kinds of cars we build, whether we salvage the railroads — those decisions are not being made in the national interest. They're being made in the short-term interests of the people who own capital. Who decides that Chrysler will build gas guzzlers? We don't vote on that, although you can bet we get stuck with the bill. The reason they build big cars is not because that's what people want, but because on a per car basis they can make a bigger profit. Why did the oil companies abandon American oil fields in favor of those in the Middle East, leaving us prone to the kind of crisis we face today? Because their charts showed that profits would be twice as high on foreign oil. Incidentally, that's what the companies are supposed to do.

John Sweringen, chief executive officer of Standard Oil of Indiana, recently said in a published interview: 'We're not in the energy business. We're in the business of trying to use the assets entrusted to us by our shareholders to give them the best return on the money they've invested in the company'. Which is fine, that *is* their job. But why let *them* define the national energy policy? Which is what they now do through their surrogates in government. Clearly, it would be in the national interest for Mobil to use its huge profits to look for oil and produce it. The oil companies would much rather buy up the rest of the economy. After all, they're the only firms benefiting from the energy crisis. Who asked Mobil to buy Montgomery Ward? They decided it was more in *their* interest.

No one in the established parties is even willing to touch the central question: Shall we govern the instruments of production in the U.S. in our interest or in the interest of the people who happen to own the capital and make the profits?

A few months back, Paul Volcker, chairman of the Federal Reserve Bank, went before Congress and made an astonishing statement. 'Under these [current economic] conditions, the standard of living of the average American has to decline'. The statement itself is not all that explosive; businessmen, bankers and corporate executives have been saying that for some time. What was astonishing was that not a single political figure — no republican or democrat, not Carter or Kennedy or Brown — rose up to challenge him.

Q.     Actually is that all that bad? Do we need all those hot tubs and snowmobiles?

A.     That's not what Volcker was talking about. The people who can afford those luxuries will still be able to afford them. What he said was that there's no way to run the economic system without making it harder for the average person in this country to live. And you know what? As things are currently run, he's absolutely right.

Do you realize that in the last 10 years, the rate of increase in the U.S. economy has been the lowest of all industrialized countries in the world? We have a stagnant economy, and what Volcker was saying was that under these circumstances, we have to suppress the standard of living.

There was a time when private enterprise in America helped the country. For example, when Edison, Ford and Firestone made their inventions, it improved productivity. Even when General Motors put in the fast assembly line — yes, it was bad for the workers, but — it did raise the overall standard of living. Those old ways of raising productivity no longer work.

Q.      How would you raise productivity now?

A.      By fostering a photovoltaic industry; by encouraging farmers to develop gasohol and assuring them that Detroit will manufacture cars that will be able to use it; by rebuilding the railroads; and by embarking on a massive, long-term solar transition. Look at the railroads, the most efficient way to transport cargo cross-country, and we're watching them die because no one can make a profit on them. Every European country has better railroads than we have. They all run at a loss, but they do help the economy as a whole. And even we have nonprofit national services that no one objects to — the Army, for example. There are ways of increasing productivity, reducing unemployment and raising the standard of living, but they are in conflict with decisions based on the profit motive.

It's time to say: Let's do things, not in the interest of profit, but in the interest of national welfare. Let's begin to assert social governance over the means of production.

Q.      Just how do you propose to bring this change?

A.      Well, for starters we have to abandon any thought of working within the two established parties. Both the Democratic and Republican parties are committed to not talking about the

*54*

alternatives to the free market. It isn't even that they're for it, they just don't want to talk about it.

That's one reason nobody votes any more, turnout dips further with each election, because there's seldom any reason to vote. When was the last time you were happy to be voting *for* somebody rather than disgusted that you had to be voting *against* somebody?

Q.    A few months back, I would have had to ask you about Kennedy or Brown in this context but their candidacies have faded. Surprisingly, John Anderson is the one who's mounted the challenge. How do you evaluate him?

A.    The only thing that's surprising about Anderson is the tenacity with which the liberal media and establishment have suddenly taken to clutching him to their hearts. There's no question that he's a decent, honest man. But there's something to what Studs Terkel said last night at the rally; "People are so tired of dealing with these two-foot midgets that you give them somebody who's two feet four and they start proclaiming him a giant."

Look, the guy's a republican, and that's no accident. There was an article in this morning's *Los Angeles Times* surveying his voting record. It pointed out that the U.S. Chamber of Commerce has given Anderson a higher rating than 73 percent of House republicans and that only eight percent of the democrats were rated higher. Meanwhile, the AFL-CIO rated Anderson higher than 69 percent of House republicans, but gave 94 percent of the democrats a better rating. In other words, there are something like three hundred people in the House alone who are more 'liberal,' more worker-oriented, than Anderson. So this love affair is something of a mystery.

Listen to what he's saying: He says we have to discipline ourselves, that we can't both increase our military budget and decrease our income tax. In other words, he favors increased military spending. Or consider his much-vaunted energy proposal, the 50 cent per gallon tax surcharge on gasoline. It's true, he's somewhat courageous in hazarding a proposal like that. He's also dead wrong, because increasing the price of fuel inevitably places a regressive burden on the poor.

Now, Anderson includes all these fancy ways of turning that 50 cents back over to the poor, (social-security tax cuts and so forth), but he fails to understand that when you increase gas by 50 cents, it's not just gas. You're hiking prices throughout the economy — tomatoes go up, grapefruit, paper, steel, automobiles — everything. The way to deal with inflation and lagging productivity is by stabilizing energy prices, not ballooning them. Anderson is unprepared to consider the kind of measures that could bring about such a stabilization. And, by the way, the same goes for Carter with his 10 cent fee on imported oil.

There's some talk of Anderson mounting an independent candidacy this year should he lose the republican nomination. I think it would be a sad mistake for liberals to support such a venture, and not just because of Anderson's false liberalism. It's time we stopped indulging in these futile one-shot protest candidacies and began building toward taking actual power. The only excuse for an independent candidacy this year is as a launching platform for a long-term effort to build a new party.

Q. Would you be willing to be the presidential candidate of the Citizens party in 1980?

A. That's not really the point. One of the things we're trying to do in the Citizens party is to down-play the emphasis on personalities and instead return the focus to the issues. For the time being, our party's task is to secure a place on as many state ballots as possible so that we'll be there in November. As far as the particular candidate goes, that will be decided by the membership later on down the line.

Incidentally, when you talk with me you mainly hear about energy issues, because that's what I know best. Talk with some of these others, and you'll hear more about other Citizens party concerns.

Q. But you're generally regarded as the most likely candidate.

A. Well, we'll see how things look later in the year. I'll tell you one thing though, since you ask. A lot of people have been coming up to me and saying, "Come on, you've got a good reputation, you don't want to get involved in politics." And I start to think, You know, that's true...

But then I have to say, wait a minute, what does this mean? It means that the process that's supposed to operate this democracy smells bad and you shouldn't get near it. Well, some of us are going to have to stick our necks out and work hard to turn politics into something worth doing and get this thing off the ground. But the only way to do it is for people to start to organize.

Q. As a mental exercise, what is the darkest vision you have of the next 10 years?

A. I refuse to have dark visions.

Q. What if the Citizens party should fail to consolidate itself? The business round table is clearly consolidating itself, the right is on the move, the war lobby is on the move...

A. We'll have fascism. The economic establishment seriously believes that they're going to carry through a program of austerity and economic retrogression, but they're going to have to do so over the opposition of enormous numbers of people in this country. The unions won't like it, poor people and minorities won't like it. How do you think they'll succeed against that kind of opposition? There's only one way, by dictatorship, by fascism. I think the economic motivations are there. I think that's what John Connally represents.

Q. But conversely, isn't there a parallel danger should the Citizens party and its program begin to gain wide adherence? Do you think the corporations are simply going to give up?

A. No, I think that if the policies of the Citizens party began to be put into effect, there would be serious opposition from corporations. But I think they would be on the defensive against a popular majority that was dealing not with superficialities, but with real basic issues. You know, the corporations have never been confronted with a situation where, so to speak, the game was up. When confronted with the reality of popular democracy, I think you'll be surprised to see how many corporate executives throw in the towel.

Q. We've seen how American corporations handled the reality of such a popular democracy in, for example, Chile.

A.      Yeah, but there they had an outside vehicle, the CIA, to do their bidding. The point is, this challenge would be taking place in America itself, and there wouldn't be any outside recourse. Sure, it's a problem.

I don't think there would necessarily be a right wing *coup d'etat* should the Citizens party win a national election; because what the Citizens party is addressing is the country's basic mission of looking after its own people, and that's a goal a lot of businessmen share. If we can show that we have a better way of doing that than the democrats or republicans, many of them will come around.

Besides, what's the alternative? If you say that the defeat of a movement for economic democracy like the Citizens party would mean fascism, and then you turn around and say that its victory would also mean fascism, what do you do then? Say 'forget it' and drop out? No, I think the only historic step that can be taken is to move in the direction of economic democracy, and then you face the next battle as it arises.

*Excerpt from the book,*

# The Other Candidates: Third Parties in Presidential Elections
*University Press of New England; 1983*
*by*
*Frank Smallwood*

## The Citizens Party

In the spring of 1979, a group of dissident liberals who were disillusioned with Jimmy Carter's presidency began exploratory discussions about the feasibility of organizing a new political party. The movement gained momentum, and in December 1979 an organizing committee filed papers with the Federal Election Commission to establish the Citizens party.

The party had its founding convention in Cleveland, Ohio, in April 1980, with author Studs Terkel serving as convener. Representatives from 32 states attended the convention, where they nominated Barry Commoner for president and LaDonna Harris for vice-president.

Although the party experienced difficulty raising funds as a result of its late start, it did receive a number of endorsements from former-Attorney General Ramsey Clark, former-Oklahoma senator and 1976 democratic presidential aspirant; Fred Harris (the husband of La-Donna Harris); and William Winpisinger, president of the International Association of Machinists. The party, which appeared on the ballot in 30 states, received 234,294 votes, with over one-quarter of the total coming from California.

Commoner, a 62 year old biologist and international spokesman on environmental issues, has authored many books, including *The Closing Circle* (1971), *The Poverty of Power* (1976), and *The Politics of Energy* (1979). LaDonna Harris was the 49 year old president of *Americans for Indian Opportunity.* I interviewed Barry Commoner in his office in the Center for the Biology of Natural Systems at Queens College in New York in late June 1981. He offered the following comments on his involvement with the Citizens party. "I'm a congenital optimist...I'm absolutely convinced that 1980 will be looked on as the first year of a new political realignment in this country."

Barry Commoner
Personal Background

Smallwood: I'd like to start with a little background information. When and how did you first get involved in politics?

Commoner: My approach to politics has been through the route of what you might call the responsibility of the scientist. I was always interested in science. I was born in Brooklyn, and I received my undergraduate education at Columbia and my graduate education at Harvard. In 1942, after I had taught biology for a couple of years at Queens College, I went into the Navy. Although I was only 25 years old at the time, I became engaged in a number of interesting assignments which clarified the public implications of science. The last assignment I had was as the Navy's liaison with the Senate Military Service Committee. I was intimately involved in writing the National Science Foundation bill in its original form, and I also participated in organizing the first hearings when Robert Oppenheimer testified immediately after the release of the information on the Manhattan District (atomic bomb) project. This early involvement reinforced my feelings, as a professional scientist, that we have a social responsibility which goes beyond just doing our own work, because of the enormous social implications of modern scientific research.

Smallwood: Did you become actively involved in politics after you left the service?

Commoner: No, not immediately, but after the war, I became very active in dealing with a variety of social issues. Before joining the faculty at Washington University in St. Louis, I worked for a year as associate editor of *Science Illustrated* which gave me a background in the public information dimensions of science and education. I spent many years in the Scientists' Institute for Public Information and in the American Association for the Advancement of Science, working with people like Margaret Mead, and getting social issues discussed by scientific groups. What I'm saying is that my concern, with social and political issues, is very long-standing. However, my earlier concerns were focused more on public education than on active politics.

Smallwood: What influenced you to help organize the new Citizens party?

Commoner: The question of why my own activity in this area shifted from analysis and public education into the creation of a new political party is described in the last chapter of my latest book, *The Politics of Energy.*[1] What I have been doing in recent years is to look for such problems as the energy crisis and the environmental crisis. I've ended up concluding that the reasons have to do with the governance of production decisions: who decides how we use our resources; what we produce and how we produce it. The crucial issue is what I call democratic social governance of the means of production. The decisions should not be made in the interests of maximizing private profits. This is the most critical issue of our era, and it requires a whole new approach to politics.

I'm involved in politics because its become crystal clear that the issues I've been concerned with — nuclear issues, environmental issues, energy issues — are not going to be solved simply by protest. We have to make some fundamental changes in our production system. In order to make these changes, we're going to have to develop a new approach to politics in this country.

---

[1] Barry Commoner, *The Politics of Energy*, 1st Ed., New York; Knopf, 1979.

Political Ideology

Smallwood: Could you clarify this new approach? What changes do you advocate, and why do these changes involve the creation of an entirely new political party?

Commoner: I think the first point is to analyze the country's political situation in such a way as to discover what political vehicle is appropriate to the new situation; whether or not a third party is needed. A lot of people say third parties will not succeed, but I think the reason why they haven't succeeded, with the one exception of the Republican party back in 1860, is that there has never been an adequate analysis of the political/economic reasons for third parties. When an issue that confronts the country becomes so profound that discussing it threatens the possibility of winning elections, the major parties shy away from it. The best example in the past is the slavery issue. If you'll look at the history of the campaigns that preceded the election of Lincoln, you'll find what historians call 'the ignominious period of American politics'. This was the period in which we elected all the presidents whose names you don't remember: Harrison, Tyler, Polk, Taylor, Fillmore, Pierce and Buchanan. The question is: Why did we have this rash of nonentities as presidents? The answer is: They were carefully chosen as nonentities because none of the political parties wanted to discuss slavery in a national campaign for fear of losing the election. It was too hot to handle, too difficult an issue. When Lincoln prepared his Lincoln-Douglas debate speech, he wrote into it opposition to the extension of slavery. But his friends advised him to steer clear of this because they said he'd lose votes. He did not follow their advice; he opposed extension of slavery, and of course, he lost that election. The creation of the Republican party was really almost forced on the country by the abdication of politics by the whigs and the democrats who were not willing to deal with the slavery issue. That explains why the Republican party grew so fast.

Smallwood: Do you think a similar situation exists in the United States today?

Commoner: Generalizing from this historical experience, I believe that a third party is called for when the two major parties are incapable of confronting critical issues and conduct charades instead of campaigns. That's exactly the situation we have in America today. There is an enormous amount of evidence that the American people are turning away from both the democrats and the republicans: the declining participation in elections, and the fact that issues aren't discussed in campaigns. This is the analysis that led to the creation of the Citizens party.

The reason for the collapse of two party politics is that there is a fundamental issue facing the country that neither party is willing to touch because of their unquestioning acceptance of the basic premises of capitalism. In particular, that the owner of the capital is free to decide how to use it, what to produce and how to produce it, on the sole criterion of maximizing profit. But, it is no longer in the national interest for production decisions to be made on this single criterion, never asking what's good for the country, what will create jobs, what will protect the environment, what will conserve energy. The new Citizens party believes that from now on these decisions are going to have to be made in the national interest. This is what I mean by social governance of the means of production, a position which is obviously contradictory to the basic premise of the capitalistic economic system. I think that the two major parties are afraid to discuss almost any issue because just below the surface is this one. For example, any deep analysis of the energy question leads to the fact that our dependence on foreign oil was brought about by the oil companies because it maximized their profits.

So the first thing is the analysis. A lot of people thought that those of us who were involved with creating the Citizens party were just another one of these spasms trying to create a third party — a People's party, the Wallace thing, and so on. A sort of 'here we go again' politics. This is far from the truth. Those of us who decided to create a new party acted on the basis of the rationale I've just described, in the conviction that it *had* to be done. That was the first step.

Smallwood: It appears that the central thrust of the Citizens party is the corporate power issue. What are your proposed remedies? Do you advocate public control of the energy industries, the multinationals, and the large corporations?

Commoner: You're right on target. The key word is control, which is a very flexible concept. I mean we followed a kind of principle of political parsimony. For example, if the issue is social control of the production decisions, that does not necessarily require social ownership. What you look for is the simplest way to achieve control. We are basically in favor of public control of the structure of the economy. But you can achieve this in a lot of different ways depending on the circumstances. You can achieve this without telling a local ice cream parlor what flavor ice cream to sell. In cases like this, you don't need public ownership.

In other cases, however, it may be impossible to achieve control without ownership. For example, take the railroads. Since they certainly make lower profits than other enterprises, what capitalist would want to own them? So we came out for nationalizing the railroads. On the other hand, with respect to the oil companies, a different form of control might be appropriate. We discussed that in the Citizens party through position papers and so on, and the simplest way of doing it would be to set up a federal energy corporation that would take complete control over import, production, and distribution of energy. Now does that mean nationalization? Not necessarily. For example, the government could write contracts with various oil companies to produce oil in Texas and sell it at a fixed price, making the oil companies public utilities. Nothing very strange about that.

Smallwood: How does your position differ from the older parties on the left — for example, the Socialist party?

Commoner: We developed our positions quite empirically in contrast with any of the socialist parties. We were not being guided by what you might call a historic theory. Clearly we understood what socialism calls for, public ownership and control of the means of production. We stressed control, the problem is that you have social ownership without adequate social control. I regard our position as a very valuable idea. I still think this is exactly what the world is about. It seems to me that the campaign worked. There is no question about it. With very little support — we had no brain trust to speak of, just a few of us with the idea in our heads — we could go from one local situation to another and made a hell of a lot of sense out of it.

Smallwood: Wouldn't the system of public control you're advocating require a lot of money? How do you plan to get the funds to support this concept?

Commoner: It's self-evident. We should make productive use of government funds that are now being wasted on foolish military expenditures. Military spending has zero productivity. It's ridiculous. We should take that money and put it into productive outlets, rebuilding the railroads and other socially useful activities. Its obvious that we have the money if we want to spend it this way.

Smallwood: In terms of your political ideology, you've placed a lot of emphasis on economic issues and corporate control. What about other social issues such as equal opportunity and the like? Is the Citizens party a single-issue group?

Commoner: No, no. Not at all. The corporate power issue is related to every other issue. Take the problems of racial and sexual discrimination. Of course in both cases there are psychological, social and institutional issues involved. But I believe that the driving force is economic. Both blacks and women get 40 percent less pay than whites and men. Why is this the case? It means that the corporations are making that much more profit. We argue that we've got to exercise control over the corporations to prevent this type of discrimination. As I said in my campaign, the old idea that what's good for General Motors is good for the country, has to be changed. The public must get control over its economic destiny in order to deal with these social issues.

The guiding principle is that the multifarious problems in the country — where we are dealing with the environment, energy, racial discrimination, sexual discrimination, the decay of the cities, any one of these things — go back to a fundamental fault. They're all connected to the basic problem that the resources of this country are not used in the peoples' interest. They are managed, used (or rather, misused), and guided by the single criterion of maximizing a corporation's profits. It would be a blooming miracle if the thousands and thousands of production decisions that have determined how the country lives, all of which are being made on the criterion of maximizing profits, happened to turn out to be good for women, blacks, children and so on. But they don't. They turn out to be good for the corporations. Any one of these issues is related to this very fundamental power of the corporations. This is what we have tried to explain in the campaign, based on the intellectual pattern that had been worked out.

## The 1980 Campaign

Smallwood: Tell me a little about the 1980 campaign.

Commoner: Let's start with the creation of the Citizens party. A small group of us began preliminary discussions in 1979. It was a marvelous dialectic. We decided that we had to have a new party to deal with the country's problems but there was a big disagreement whether we should be involved in the 1980 presidential campaign at all. Wouldn't it be better to develop local parties and maybe four years from now build up to a national campaign? It was a very lively debate, and those of us who felt we ought to have a national campaign won.

Once some of us decided we wanted to create a new party, we formed an organizing group — about one hundred people — which we called the Citizens Committee. Members were recruited from what you might call the public interest constituency: environmental groups, some rank and file union leaders, and people interested in energy and the decentralization of resources. The idea was that these types of people would be our national constituents.

Smallwood: Did this committee organize the new Citizens party?

Commoner: Yes. The first job we faced was to create the party in compliance with the federal election laws because our long-range hope — an extreme hope you might say — was that if we got five percent of the vote, we would then be entitled to federal matching funds. According to our reading of the federal election laws, only a regularly organized party receiving five percent of the vote would qualify for matching funds. So we went to great lengths to conform to the requirements of the federal law as to what is a party. For example, there had to be a national convention, we had to organize a certain number of state groups, and the like. We did all of that in order to be sure that we qualified. One of the great ironies of the 1980 campaign was that Anderson qualified for matching funds even though he clearly did not conform to the election laws because he did not establish a political party. That was one of the great bitter ironies of the campaign.

Somehow we did organize the party. It was an enormous job. We had to have a national convention far too early in our young life. It was held in Cleveland in April 1980, since we couldn't delay it — which would have been smart. My guess is between three hundred to five hundred people attended the national convention. I would say half of them had been members of the Citizens party for less than a few weeks. At that point, there was no real communion of ideas, but we had to have it that early because we had to nominate our candidates in order to get on the ballot. In fact, one of the problems we faced was that the Ohio law required that we have our candidates nominated in March. This led to all kinds of difficulties, because we were very much concerned with internal democracy. The question arose in March as to whether I would respond to a request of the Ohio party and declare that I was a candidate for president, even though we hadn't had our convention and we hadn't democratically decided whether I or someone else should be a candidate. So, we held our convention in April, and LaDonna Harris and I were nominated.

Smallwood: I'm not entirely clear exactly where the party stood at this point. Did you adopt a platform at your convention?.

Commoner: Let me tell you about the platform. One of the problems the Citizens party has wrestled with from the very beginning is internal democracy. The people who were instrumental in the first organization of the party were convinced that we had to be different from all other political parties and have very strong internal democracy. So the decision was made that the convention would adopt a draft platform based on input from all of the local parties. Position papers and resolutions were sent in on the theory that a draft platform would be constructed at the convention which would then be voted on by the entire membership of the party by mail. It was an insane idea, which utterly failed, — utterly. In the first place, what we got out of the convention was such a mishmash of contradictory opinions and contradictory ideas, that it took a committee of six people a week, locked up in a room in Washington, just to make a three hundred-item program out of that. There were completely bizarre things like abolishing the border between Mexico and the

United States. The upshot was that the committee in Washington produced this thing, about three hundred items, some of which were alternatives which were sent out to the membership for voting. That happened some time in late summer. I don't know how many members voted, but it was a complete bust. The huge three hundred-item platform was never officially adopted. What happened instead was that the state groups would write their own, very brief pointed platforms which explained what we stood for.

Smallwood: I'm sorry, but I find this confusing. Did the party adopt a consistent central position, or did you present your own positions on the issues?

Commoner: That's right, that came out of discussions in the executive committee. We learned as we went along. And let me tell you, you're a professor, did the students ever come up to you after class and say, "that was an interesting lecture, but let me tell you how to improve it next time?" That doesn't happen to you in class, right? It didn't happen to me in class, either. But when I started campaigning that was an everyday occurrence. I was their property. I gave pretty good speeches, and people would come up to me and say, "Well now, you know the way you put that position on the women's question, that's not good." They would write me long letters. It was quite a shock to find that people didn't say, "Gee, that was a great speech." They'd say, "That was a pretty good speech, but I think you can do better." It's still true. Yesterday I spoke at a rally, and the head of the New York Citizens party said to me, "Hey, that was pretty good, that was the best speech you've given in recent weeks." It was a powerful experience and forced me to learn how best to present the party's position in ways that made sense to its members and supporters.

Smallwood: After the April convention was over, did you start to campaign right away?

Commoner: No. The first enormous job we faced was trying to get on the ballot in the different states. Most of our financial resources were used up in that effort, and we came out of the ballot access campaign with practically no money at all. We attempted to get on the different state ballots through completely local effort because, as you know, the federal election laws are not national, they're local. The way we did it was by locating half a dozen people in each state who looked as if they were interested in organizing the party. We called them the conveners of the state party. They would then get together and find a lawyer who would figure out what the state laws required. The task was enormously variable. It only takes eight hundred signatures to get on the ballot in New Jersey, but several hundred thousand in California. All kinds of queer things. They would work it out on the local level, and then it was their responsibility to get the party on the ballot. We gave them a certain amount of legal help. We had some lawyers who would help their local lawyers. We followed this up with visits by LaDonna Harris and myself in different states to encourage people to join the party and participate in the ballot access campaign.

Beginning in April, I spent an awful lot of time just traveling around making speeches in order to help the local party groups organize to get us on the ballot. And we did pretty well. We also spent some money in getting full time people to go out and collect signatures because the time was so short that very often that was the only way in which it could be done. It's a very difficult logistical problem to collect signatures. A lot of people think you just go out and ask friends to sign a petition, but when you need a lot of signatures, it just can't be done that way. You have to figure out exactly where the people are and where they'll be moving slowly enough so they'll sign something.

Smallwood: So, in effect you were sort of learning through experience?

Commoner: That's right. I still remember the opening of the petition campaign here in New York. I agreed to participate in the opening festivities, and I traveled out to Long Island somewhere. The idea was that I was going to campaign through a commuter train, but of course, it was so jammed you couldn't move, so that was that. Then we got to Penn Station. The big campaign signature collection was to be at the mouth of Penn Station at rush hour. It was the most amazing scene in the world. We had people standing there, and they were like rocks in a rushing stream, with people just whizzing past them. Nobody wanted to stop and sign petitions. Finally, we looked around and across the street there was a line at a bus stop. Some of us went over there and finally we got some signatures. Of course, the people there were standing still waiting for the next bus. It took us a little time to learn where you go for signatures. There was a lot to be learned. I think it's remarkable that we got on thirty state ballots, which is a record for a really new, independent party on its first time out. I think the libertarians only got on two state ballots in their first election. What we did was to create the local parties; and the campaign was run by the local parties as well. There was no national campaign in the sense that we had a national headquarters that sent out advance people and publicity. Hundreds of election materials were published, fascinating posters, leaflets, brochures, not one of them published by the national party, all done locally. It was an amazing thing. By the end of July or August, we had functioning state and local groups, and they did the campaigning.

Smallwood: How did you organize your own campaign schedule under such a decentralized arrangement?

Commoner: The national office did my scheduling. They scheduled LaDonna Harris and me to go out and speak; they planned ways of raising money and that was about it. We didn't even have a national press secretary until October. The schedule was set up and I would travel, half the time alone or sometimes with one person helping me. I would come into the next town and the local schedule was completely organized by the local people. They decided where to have the press conferences, fund-raisers or rallies. I simply did my thing, and then went off to another town. What may surprise you is that those activities were uniformly successful. The rallies were jammed, we got good local press coverage. You probably didn't see any of that unless you visited a town where we were. I remember a day in Grand Rapids, Michigan. There was live local television coverage of a press conference we held at noon. We were on the front page of the newspaper. There was good local coverage. The coverage we didn't get was from the big television networks and the major national newspapers. That was devastatingly harmful, no question about it.

Smallwood: Why do you think you were virtually ignored by the television networks and the major national newspapers?

Commoner: It's very simple. I'll tell you why exactly. This is a true story. In Albuquerque, New Mexico, I was interviewed by a reporter, and he said to me, 'Dr. Commoner, I want to ask you an impertinent question. Are you really a serious candidate or are you just running on the issues?' I'm not kidding! That's literally what he said, and this is the explanation of the behavior of the big media.

I met the editorial board of the *New York Times*. I met with the editorial board of the *Washington Post* as well as with a number of other newspapers. It had zero impact on anything they did. The reason is — you ask any of them — you go and talk with them — the only thing they regard as serious is your chance of being elected. The reason Anderson was given coverage is that there was some chance that he might have been elected. I had no intention of being elected. It was obvious that I wasn't going to be elected. The result was that the major news media participated in making the campaign a charade in which the real issues were avoided. I can be pretty bitter about it because the galling thing is that the predicament we're in now, in which we elected Reagan to office without making the consequences at all clear to the country, can be laid at the door of the media. Did you see the recent CBS broadcast on war and defense? It opened up with the statement that this is a terribly important issue which no one is discussing, and then it shows Reagan during the campaign making these wild claims about the military and so on. This was never really discussed in the campaign. Why in God's name didn't they do this type of broadcast during the campaign?

Smallwood: So your major problem was with the national media?

Commoner: Yes. We received practically no coverage from the networks. I finally got on the phone and made some appointments with the vice-presidents in charge of news and met with Bud Benjamin of CBS, and with Les Crystal of NBC. The other major network, ABC, refused to meet for quite a while until I pressed them. The upshot was that CBS and NBC sent crews out to cover us for several days when I made speeches about nuclear war and other crucial issues. What they showed was a four-minute sequence of me getting in and out of private cars to indicate that I didn't have Secret Service protection. There was practically no substantive coverage. At ABC they didn't even do that. When I met with them, I said, "You know, the issues are not being discussed in this campaign. It's up to you to show that some of us are discussing the issues." And they said,

"Yeah, yeah, that's an interesting idea." One of them turned to the other and said, 'We ought to do a program on that after the campaign.' I know from the reporters at the *Washington Post* and the *New York Times* who did cover us that they tried very hard to get assigned on a long-term basis, but they were held back by their editors. Finally, they were given a chance to go on one trip or something like that. You should talk with some of the reporters. It was disappointing.

Personal Impressions

Smallwood: In spite of your disappointment, it seems to me you can claim some solid accomplishments. You got on the ballot in 30 states. You began to build a state and local party organization. Where do you think the Citizens party is going in the years ahead?

Commoner: Well, in the first place, you have to take a look at what the campaign taught us about our constituency. I've got a county-by-county record of our vote which is very interesting. It turns out that our strength lay not where we thought it was, not in the highly politically organized places like New York City and Detroit. Our strongest votes were in outlying areas. In four counties in Appalachia in the western part of Virginia, we beat Anderson. I didn't even know about it because we had not had a Citizens party there. In January, I went down to speak at Emory and Henry College which is in southwestern Virginia just above the Tennessee border. After the election, I discovered that we had gotten a very considerable vote down there, around eight percent. As a result, some people put an ad in the local papers and said let's organize a Citizens party. That turns out to be a very significant aspect of the pattern of our vote. For example, take Burlington, Vermont. As you know, we ran four candidates for the city council in April 1981; and as I recall the figures, one of them won with 60 percent of the vote. The other three averaged 30 percent of the vote.* We also helped elect a coalition socialist candidate, Bernie Sanders, as mayor of Burlington. You're familiar with him? Now people may say, "Well, that's only Burlington,

---

*Citizens party candidates won additional seats on the Burlington City Board of Aldermen in the March 1982 elections.

Vermont." Yet that's the kind of place where I think our strength lies.

Smallwood: Do you think the party's future strength may come from the small cities and rural areas?

Commoner: Here's what's going on. Take a city like Detroit where we had a strong party effort, and a very difficult task of getting on the ballot, which we did. After we got on the ballot, however, we were just one of a number of very highly organized political groups. You know, every one of the political splinter groups is very active in Detroit. They're all highly organized, which made it hard for our party to find a way to move. So that's one point.

The second point is that we misjudged our base of support. What we thought was our natural constituency, the public interest organizations, turned out *not* to be the big supporters of our organization. We made a fundamental mistake here. In hindsight, you can see why, though we didn't realize it at the time. The public interest groups are interested in lobbying people who are in power. When I got up and said I wasn't going to get elected, why should they vote for me?, I was saying that I wasn't going to be there to be lobbied. These groups are in a certain sense symbiotically related to the conventional political power base. The people who supported us were what you might call the autonomous, independently-minded voters who are not in organizations. Who are they? Miners, farmers and craftspeople. In southwest Virginia I was told that our typical supporters don't like to join organizations. In other words, we had touched what you might call the historical populist base of the country. It's very interesting what's happening. We are appealing to basically unorganized voters. We also work with the unions as best we can, where people like William Winpisinger supported us very courageously.

Some critics look at us and say we only got 230,000 votes in 1980, so we're not going anywhere. But our constituency is larger. In November 1980, wherever we ran local candidates, they did much better — six to 20 percent of the vote — than the national ticket. Many people who supported the party locally ended up voting for Carter, because they were so afraid of Reagan, but we didn't expect to win this election, just as the Republican party didn't win its first election in 1856. That's not what this was all about. What we are really doing is establishing a political position for the future. I'm absolutely convinced that 1980 will be looked on as the first year of a new political realignment in this country.

Smallwood: Let me conclude with a couple of personal questions. You're an academic, a professional scientist. When I was active in state politics, I found that a lot of the social dimensions of politics involves small talk and compromise. Did you find this frustrating?

Commoner: Nope. You have to understand, I've been a public speaker for many years. I mean, I've done the university circuit, and that was part of my social responsibility as a scientist. I get a great kick out of taking my understanding of the intellectual content of the problem and making it accessible to ordinary people. I've done that with abstract scientific matters as well as political matters.

Smallwood: That's the public education function of politics, but what about all the inconsequential chitchat? The solicitation of other people? How do you feel about that?

Commoner: Oh, you mean fund raising and so on. Well, it's not particularly frustrating. I'm no good at remembering names and faces, but I just try to behave in a natural way at fund raisers, to tell people what's on my mind. I speak in a plain way. We didn't make any political deals, so that wasn't frustrating.

Smallwood: Fairly late in the campaign, in mid-October, you began running nationwide ads that included the word 'bullshit' to describe what your major opponents were saying. Doesn't this indicate a degree of frustration on your part?

Commoner: Well, the frustration was due to the failure of not getting any national publicity. Sure. But overall I have very positive feelings about the campaign.

Smallwood: O.K. Here's my last question. You spent a great deal of time and energy on this effort. Was it worth it?

Commoner: Oh, I'm very glad about it; it was a year of very intense activity, and well worth it. Personally, because my purpose was to get involved — I didn't want to run for president — that was not my intent. All I wanted to do is to create what I think the country badly needs, which is a new political party. I ran because I was convinced that this was the best way in which I could serve that purpose. It worked. It absolutely worked. We created a new political party. The ideas behind it make sense, so it certainly was worthwhile.

Anyone who's worked with me knows that I'm a congenital optimist. Of course I'm optimistic. I am, because I think this is the issue, and I think we've at last put our finger on what has to be done. I'm encouraged that as people begin to understand it, they will act on it. It's very gratifying to find that there are people whose whole approach to politics has been changed by the ideas that we have developed, and come the next election, *Time* magazine is going to be surprised to discover that several hundred left-wingers have been elected to local office.

There's something going on. It shows that where you don't have the dead hand of the paralyzed political establishment, people are moving. So I don't think for a minute that the country was turned to the right. There's no evidence of that whatsoever. Sure, the republicans and the right-wingers have gotten smart about raising money and using television, but there is a very deep-seated sense of progressivism in the country. We might end up merging with a labor party — who knows. But we have managed to show that it is possible to create an independent political party on the basis of an integrated set of ideas that are not handed in some prepackaged political formula. As I told you earlier, I'm absolutely convinced that 1980 will be looked on as the first new year of a new political alignment in this country.

## Funding

The only third party or independent candidate who received any federal funding, in 1980, was John Anderson, and this was a close call. Anderson qualified for $4.2 million in retroactive federal funds after he received 5,720,060 popular votes, or 6.6 percent of the total cast in the 1980 presidential election (thus surpassing the required five percent). However, Anderson only received these funds after the election was already over, and after he had already raised over $10 million in private contributions and loans. None of the other third party candidates received any federal funds at all.

Each of the candidates was required to report his or her total expenditures to the Federal Election Commission. Anderson led the list by reporting total campaign expenses of $14,979,141. The second largest third party expenditure of $3,210,763 was reported by the libertarians, with over two million of this coming from the party's vice-presidential nominee, David Koch, a wealthy New York chemical engineer who was permitted by law to contribute an unlimited amount to his own campaign[1]. The other third party candidates spent considerably less than either Anderson or Clark; none of them reported expenses of more than two hundred thousand dollars to finance his or her 1980 presidential campaigns. The complete list of expenditures reported to the FEC by all eleven of the third party and independent candidates who ran in two or more states in 1980 is as follows:[2]

| | |
|---|---:|
| John Anderson (Independent) | $14,979,141 |
| Ed Clark (Libertarian) | 3,210,763 |
| Gus Hall (Communist) | 194,775 |
| Andrew Pulley (Socialist Workers) | 186,257 |
| Ellen McCormack (Right-to-Life) | 81,101 |
| Deirdre Griswold (Workers World) | 39,772 |
| David McReynolds (Socialist) | 38,180 |
| Barry Commoner (Citizens) | 23,411 [3] |
| John R. Rarick (American Independent) | 13,932 |
| Percy Greaves (American) | 13,488 |
| Benjamin Bubar (National Statesman) | 890 |
| | $18,781,710 |

---

[1] *Dollar Politics*, p.101 For a commentary on the financial problems of the third party candidates during the 1980 campaign, see Rhodes Cook, "Money Woes Limit Anderson, Third Party Presidential Bids," *Congressional Quarterly*, August 16, 1980, pp.23w74-78

[2] The third party expenditure totals, reported to the FEC by the candidates' principal campaign committees, were obtained from the Public Records Office, Federal Election Commission, 1325 K Street, Washington, D.C., in January 1982. The reports cover expenditures through December 1980.

[3] As Barry Commoner explained in his interview, the Citizens party ran a decentralized series of state campaigns. Under the FECA legislation, state political parties can spend unlimited amounts. The $23,411 figure represents national party (central office) expenses, and presumably the Citizens party spent more than this amount on a state-by-state basis.

The figures on the previous page make it obvious that none of these candidates, except Anderson and possibly Clark, had the financial resources necessary to gain the more than 4.3 million popular votes required to qualify for retroactive federal funds under the five percent cutoff threshold. Hence, as was previously noted, they had to comply with all of the restrictions of the FEC legislation with no real hope of gaining any federal funds in return.

# PART II

## How and Why the Media Kept the Formation of a New American Political Party a Secret from the Voting Public

Summary: Alexander Cockburn of the *Nation*, Tom Wicker of the *New York Times* and Jack Nelson of the *Los Angeles Times* are interviewed by Jeffrey Gale. The journalists respond to frank questioning about why the media ignored a candidate whose party's platform dealt directly with the issues of the day. The responses are honest in revealing that the media has become a decision-maker. Barry Commoner, Citizens party candidate in 1980, reveals the frustrations related to the media's refusal to cover his campaign.

# Presidential Election Results

## *From* Parade *Magazine, July 19, 1981*

By virtue of his victory in the 1980 presidential election, does Ronald Reagan have a mandate to spread his conservative philosophy so it embraces the entire public?

The fact is that only 53.95 percent of this country's eligible voters cast ballots in the last presidential election. This was the lowest turnout since 1948, when only 51.1 percent voted in the election that saw underdog Democratic President Harry S. Truman defeat the Republican candidate, Thomas E. Dewey.

In the 1980 election, in which 86,512,398 Americans cast their votes, Reagan got 43,903,198 (50.75%) to beat democratic incumbent Jimmy Carter, who got 35,482,796 votes (41.01%).

There were 21 presidential candidates in the 1980 election. Independent John Anderson won 5,719,715 votes (6.61%) and finished third; Libertarian party candidate Ed Clark received 921,257 votes (1.06%) and finished fourth; and Barry Commoner of the Citizens party finished fifth with 234,280 votes (0.27%).

The highest turnout in percentage terms of eligible U.S. Voters occurred in the presidential election of 1960. That was the cliffhanger in which 62.8 percent voted and Democrat John F. Kennedy defeated Richard M. Nixon by only 118,574 popular votes. Kennedy received 34,226,731 votes to Nixon's 34,108,157. It was so close that the result was in doubt until the day after the election.

# "Rules of the Game"
# Part 4: "Is There a Better Way?"

## Alexander Cockburn and James Ridgeway
### Rolling Stone, *November 13, 1980*

This has not been a year for prodigious journalistic achievement on the TV screen or in the press. There are no Norman Mailers in 1980, largely because the dramas are of a different order and the process is differently scaled. There has been no single symbolic clash this year, as there was in Chicago in 1968, or in San Francisco in 1964, when the Goldwaterites howled down Rockerfeller and Reagan made the first great speech of his republican career. There are no major stars on the journalistic circuits this time around, however deferentially the professionals may speak of a David Broder, a Lou Cannon, or a Jules Witcover.

If there is one person in the mass media who has attempted to transcend the draining, endless ritual of campaigning today, it is Bill Moyers of PBS. On the eve of the Reagan-Anderson debate, which he moderated, we talked about the press and the election.

*"Why do you think outsiders like the libertarians' Ed Clark and the Citizens party's Barry Commoner have such a hard time getting coverage on the nightly news?"* we asked.

"Because of the rules of the game, the way American politics is played," Moyers began, "it's always been basically a contest between two combatants in a game for power, not a struggle for leadership and policy in our society. So therefore the journalists who play by the rules of the game tend to exclude anyone who isn't seen to be a heavyweight contender in the main bout. Commoner, Clark or whoever, are assessed, not by the weight of their ideas, but by their standing in the traditional measurement of success or failure in American politics: *Does he have a chance to be president?*

"The traditional press does not consider ideas a force in American politics. They look for strength in numbers, chances of winning and positions. That's why they pay more attention to platforms than to other discussions between the candidates; because the platforms seem to represent positions that mainline journalists acknowledge to be what it's about. Of course that's not really true."

*"But what would happen if one of the networks stepped outside what you've just described and said to hell with it?"* we asked.

"No one knows," Moyers said, "because no one's ever done that. What keeps them in place is that willingly or unwillingly, the rules of the game require you play it that way. To answer the question you've raised, you'd really have to question the fundamental way that American politics is arranged, and then look at the whole process by which we choose presidents, and by which various candidates get considered. That means a shorter campaign, real debates, frequent presentations by the candidates to each other and not to a group of panelists. You really have to back up and start with what's wrong with American politics before you can ask the question of what is journalism doing wrong, because if the rules of the game are such, and you don't cover the game, you are off base and irrelevant. So that's why nobody does that. It's like if you play football, you don't use the rules of basketball."

*"In other words, you would be ostracized?"*
"Yes."

*"For a long time, the campaign — especially on the republican side — was about issues. Now somehow that's all been lost, don't you think?"*

"Preliminary bouts, preliminary bouts," said Moyers. "The rationale of the network executives is: We're only interested in who's going to be in the main bout, not with the visions by which the sheep are separated en route to the main bout. The only issue is who is going to win, and that's the way it's covered."

*"So what are your major suggestions for change?"*

"Take television. First of all, the political system should be structured so that you don't have to be a candidate of the two major parties to get the serious attention of the press. My theory about why Anderson went into eclipse in the summer is that the journalists covering him could not contemplate a challenge outside the two party system, and they just figured that when he didn't win the primary and didn't get a party nomination, he was through. So you would have to have an assumption in your political system that a candidate does not have to pay his dues to one of the major political parties to be seriously committed. Then, over the course of the four years prior to the election, you would have coverage of alternative views of the system, which someone — a Clark or a Commoner — might be addressing.

"I can only speak essentially to the problems I see in television covering the game, even by the rules of the game," Moyers continued. "What we need is a different game. I think we will probably not have it until this present one falls by the weight of accumulated grievances, and then from out of that chemistry, some new form will emerge. But the problem of television is simply one of time. If you only have 22 minutes in the evening to cover the world, the amount of time you give to covering a campaign becomes ridiculously small. The networks, starting at a duly appointed season, should offer an hour every week to debate, both within the parties and outside the parties. You can't do that, of course, because the networks are part of the corporate value system that governs the choices of politics and therefore the choices of coverage. I guess that's what I'm trying to get at. As long as the prevailing consensus in America is what it is politically, then it follows naturally that the prevailing method of covering that — with the exception of publications that don't have to or that deliberately do not participate in that value structure — is going to be reflected in the very narrow range of discussion that takes place."

*"How narrow can it get? Look at the way the Reagan of the primaries is already being forgotten."*

"There is no accountability for candidates running for office, except in the short memory of the press, and it's a very short memory. If the press played more of a role in looking at the institutional process of politics rather than the personality process, then Jimmy Carter would not have had a chance of being renominated. The now generally held belief — that Jimmy Carter is an unfunctioning president — would have been so obvious to an institutionalized political process that the Democratic party would not have renominated him; the party would have looked for somebody else. The institutional linkage of American politics has been wrested from its moorings, and therefore the press can only deal with the stories in those press conferences and on the trail by looking at the personal drama of the candidate. That drama shifts, so they are with Anderson when he is challenging, and they are not when he is behind; they're with Reagan when he emerges but not when he's maneuvering prior to his emergence."

# "Reduce the Military Budget," Says Commoner of the Citizens Party

## New York Times *Sunday, May 30, 1982*

Barry Commoner, co-chairman of the Citizens party, told delegates gathered for the party's national convention in New York yesterday that nothing short of large cuts in the military budget would resolve the nation's economic and social ills.

Speaking before five hundred delegates representing 30 state committees in the two-year-old political organization, Commoner said that the United States could not expect to lower interest rates, reduce unemployment or improve productivity until a commitment was made to "transfer the military budget to human needs."

"The unavoidable test for any politician who claims to favor higher domestic expenditures, lower interest rates and reduced unemployment is this: Are you willing to make a big enough cut in military budget to do it?" said Commoner, a biologist, environmentalist, and the party's presidential candidate in 1980.

Without attaching specific numbers to his proposed cuts in the arms budget, Commoner criticized the democrats for not going far enough in their proposals to cut military spending.

"The democrats claim that they want to protect the American people from the drastic cuts in domestic programs and they deride the inability of Reaganomics to reduce run-away interest rates and massive unemployment," Commoner said in his address. "But the only feasible way to deal with these problems is, in fact, precisely what neither Reagan nor the democrats is willing to propose — a massive reduction in military expenditures."

Commoner acknowledged that the Citizens party did not have a military program. Such a program was necessary, he said, to assess the country's defense spending needs. Commoner proposed a military program centered on national defense. He called for eliminating from the federal budget, all spending for nuclear war apparatus and the cost of forces for intervention in Asia, Latin America, Africa, and the Middle East. He also asked for the withdrawal of the United States' military presence in Europe.

During the three-day convention, held at the Prince George Hotel, Citizens party delegates will nominate 76 candidates for offices in 20 states for this year's elections. The party will designate candidates for 15 local offices, 40 to 50 state offices, including governors in Rhode Island and Pennsylvania, and will select candidates for 15 seats in the House of Representatives and five in the Senate.

# An Interview With
## Alexander Cockburn
*Columnist for* The Nation *and
the* Wall Street Journal, 1981
*Author of* Corruptions of Empire:
Life Studies and the Reagan Era *(Verso; 1987)*

### by
### Jeffrey Gale

Q.     Do you really feel that the media got into issues? I know you
did but I'm asking about this in a broad-spectrum way before we
discuss Barry Commoner's candidacy.

A.     There's a tendency to say that the press never, ever discusses
issues. I think that's a mistake and it's a mistake we're looking at.
The press, after all, consists of relatively well-educated people.
I mean they are not the thugs they were 50 years ago. They do
make an effort toward their responsibilities to discuss issues, but
that's only stating the problem. The question is how issues are
actually discussed. I mean, if you could go through every
newspaper in the country last year, you would find more than
once, in some pages extremely frequently, they went endlessly
into issues or what they perceived to be crucial issues in 1980.
Then you have to say, well, how are these issues actually dealt
with. Take the obvious ones, say supply side economics. I

remember when James Ridgeway and I did a long interview with Jude Wanniski in the summer of 1980 on supply side economics and the battle for Reagan's mind and so on; it sounds self-serving to say, because there was quite an influence logged that was reprinted in the *Washington Post* and the *Herald Examiner* and around the country.

Q.     That wasn't the one in *Rolling Stone* where you did the whole thing on the economy, too, was it?

A.     No, it wasn't. No this was specifically with Jude Wanniski, who is a leading publicist and a semi-theorist on supply side economics. We stated the central problems then, and I just noticed after that, papers more and more would say, in discussing the issues, "How can Reagan hope to balance the budget, pay for the defenses, and lower taxes at the same time?" Now you obviously and ultimately resolve that question by saying: 'You can't'. The issue was always stated, but it didn't become a *discussed* issue, it became: Here is a mystery question, puzzling, perplexing maybe, but never the ultimate conclusion, which is — You can't!

So, the issues are all very well-meaning. Or another obvious one is defense spending. They spend hours and hours on the *gap* — perceived gap, but it was always on the premises of the basic consensus of so-called Russian superiority in defense. With that erroneous premise they went through the various positions of Carter, Reagan, Commoner and Ed Clark. All purely symbolic statements — that's one point. The second point is, I think there were probably three occasions in the entire year — maybe two — when Reagan was seriously confronted with a question about balancing the budget.

Q.     How do you feel the national media performed in covering the 1980 presidential election as a whole — say, versus '76?

A.     Oh, much the same, I suppose. Do you mean, how did the press do?

Q.     Yes.

A.     Well, every time, they all wind up and they say: "Well, this time, we're really going to do the issues." There was a bit, in 1980, when they said: "Well, we've done the issues to death! The coverage is getting very boring" — which it was, in many ways. But I think basically, the imperatives of coverage in these national campaigns remain the same now, and the major point is the desire to get on the national news, for which they will pay, bribe or die. That remains the major incentive. You could argue, that the press went more overboard for Carter in '76 in a more abhorrent way, than they did with any candidate in 1980. The real rapture for Reagan didn't, after all, start until he was inaugurated; and many sections of the press remained dubious about Reagan.

Q.   How do you feel the national media covered Eugene McCarthy's candidacy for the presidency in 1976 when he ran as an independent, say versus the way they handled Anderson's in 1980?

A.   Oh, I think there's no doubt the coverage of Anderson was more serious and more determined. Then, of course, we could argue that Anderson was a little more popular with the established media and columnists and, indeed, was called a "creation" by many pundits, back at the beginning of 1980, or the end of 1979; unlike McCarthy, whose role in '76 was perceived as straight-forward through the splenetic sabotage.

Q.   Some people would argue that Garry Trudeau, of "Doonesbury", in certain ways, made Anderson; and no one did that for McCarthy in 1976; but that in a certain way, McCarthy's candidacy in '76 paved the way for independents like Anderson, Commoner and Clark to at least give it a run in 1980.

A.   I think McCarthy, whether you say the McCarthy of '68 or the McCarthy of '76, certainly had an enormously influential role in the treatment of people like the strategist for Anderson and for Commoner. Incidentally, on Trudeau, I think the influence of cartoonists is constantly underestimated. I think Trudeau was important with Anderson, and very important in putting down Jerry Brown, who, to my mind, was a very serious candidate — whom I liked. On the other side, I think Jeff MacNelly — just for example — made cartoons about Carter that were very damaging for Carter — extremely damaging. And you've noticed if you've read MacNelly in the papers, since Reagan won, he was very keen on Reagan, and so he has very little to say now.

Q.      Now, along the same line, young people do read "Doonesbury" to a considerable degree, yet, when you look at the vote totals, Commoner got about 230,000 votes out of a nation of 230,000,000 people. Now we know that 50 percent of the people who could have voted, stayed home. But what I am focusing on is that when you look at 230,000 votes for Commoner, that's like one giant anti-nuke rally that was held here in New York, or close to it. That's the total amount of votes he got, which leads me to believe that the media saw him as a one issue candidate. After Harrisburg, he was on "Donahue," and a lot of people phoned in and said: "Hey! Would you consider running for President?" So he ran, but the younger people didn't form an army behind him like they did for McCarthy in '68. In other words, Alex, in your opinion, why do you think the media saw him as a one issue candidate? And why wasn't he able to get an army of young people behind him in the same way that Gene McCarthy did in '68 when he dumped Lyndon Johnson?

A.      On the McCarthy question, it's very plain, that was the height of the war. And I think they'd been in Vietnam for eight years. It was increasing desperation. I wasn't in the United States at the time — I was in Europe and there was very little information. Possibly in the wake of Three Mile Island you had the same substance, in a danger, the arrogance of power, and so forth, but the desperation and fury of young people against the war in 1968 was such that McCarthy could rally them. Commoner was not really operating under the same conditions. As to the one issue candidacy thing; yes, I think he was perceived, very often, as a one issue candidate for a reason which is fairly understandable. His major issue has been nuclear power. There's Barry Commoner going around the country — he lands in some city and a reporter goes running out to meet him. A UPI guy goes out to the airport to talk to him — he looks at Barry Commoner and remembers Commoner's book, *The Closing Circle* — and he thinks, there's the prophet who knows about energy. And, I might say, in many of Commoner's statements, when he had a number of press conferences, he played the energy field extremely strongly, and then they saw him as a nuclear candidate, and that was very plain. So the premises of a single issue candidacy, although of course Commoner wasn't entirely single-issue, were there.

Q. The whole concept the Citizens party wanted to convey, it seems to me, was to get away from 'imagery and personalities' and run only an issue-oriented campaign. As you know, however, this appeared to turn the media off. Do you think the media is so conditioned to covering personalities that only someone as famous as, say, Ralph Nader, running for president in 1984 with Barry Commoner as his running mate would stand a chance outside of a two party system?

A. Well, there's an enormous number of hypotheses in the question. Obviously, a candidate has to have a personality which is to some extent striking. It has to be striking to attract the voter. You can have the best program in the world, the most serious, well thought out 240 page document, a complete economic and foreign policy program for the United States.... the libertarians did. They had vast amounts of printed material, but Ed Clark, a libertarian, did not have a particularly striking personality. He was persuasive and quite resourceful in debate, but you know, Lothario, he wasn't. Politicians reach the bulk of the American people in two minute spots, unless they're going to buy in half hours here and there. On the news, everything has to get encapsulated in terms of ideas *and* personalities. Lenin knew that very well when he invented the slogan, "Peace, Land and Bread." Slogans had to be pithy long before Walter Cronkite or Dan Rather. Obviously, the entire way politics are perceived in this country is mediated by personality and the examination of the psychology of the personality of a politician. That is without question true. For example, Ralph Nader, since 1964, has developed a relatively strong personality. He's a good speaker. He's an aggressive speaker. He learned the tricks of the media. Any candidate, whether he's from the left or the right, has to learn those tricks.

Q. Do you feel that the establishment media — with large corporate holdings on a national level — made an early decision to play down its coverage of the anti-corporate Citizens party and Dr. Barry Commoner who is a non-politician?

A.    No, I don't think so. I've spent hours talking to network executives about how decision-making is made and it's like taking a swim in cotton wool. It's very hard to find out. They are the ones who make the crucial decisions — I don't think there's a "Mister Big" on top. There could be — I'm not saying there couldn't. If a truly dangerous candidate to corporate interest appeared, and he was making a great deal of headway, I am not saying that at the very top of the network, or all of them, or at *Time* they might not make some pretty fierce decisions, to screw the guy off, either killing him by silence or killing him by smear or killing him by whatever means might come to hand. I don't think that happened in the 1980 election. I think then you're down to discussing how network news nightly producers actually perceive the flow of political events, then you come to a circular procedure: They read the papers. They read the *New York Times*; they read the *Washington Post*; they read the *Wall Street Journal*; they read the *Village Voice* and the *Nation*. They read a whole number of things. They're fairly serious citizens; and they will, on the basis of that, say: "Right, we've got 10 minutes on our network news tonight. We've got Reagan in Wisconsin attacking or speaking in favor of milk support prices; we've got Carter saying, maybe he's going to drop a bomb on Iran. We've got *x* here, and *y* there, and now we've got Barry Commoner. Okay, what are we gonna give Barry Commoner? He's launching his candidacy, there's something — a dramatic act." After awhile they're going to say: "Well, look, he's not showing in the polls. He's a blip in the polls." So then they'll drop him down a bit. Then you get the second level which are the Bill Moyers interviews. Then you get the longer term feature backup. I don't think in the case of Commoner there was a conspiracy, to answer your question directly; the guy's anti-corporate, destroy him! He never became a great enough threat for that decision.

Q.    To what extent do you feel major news organizations were influenced by the polls, in terms of how much coverage to give the candidates, and did some news agencies even go so far as to justify the amount of coverage given to make their own in-house polls seem accurate? In the old days, we only had in America, say, the Roper Poll and the Gallup Poll; now it seems like every major news organization has its own poll.

A.     Yes, of course, they're for their own polls and of course, they'll refer to the polls given their question of coverage, as with Anderson. They say he dropped from 23 to 15 to eight in the polls. Obviously if Anderson's guy rings up the networks screaming and says, "You haven't covered our candidate!" And the network guy says, "Why should we cover him? He's down to eight. Who do you think you are?" Equally, obviously, that has a reflection back on wherever the guy goes in the polls. The less he gets coverage, the less people see him, therefore, the less he's going to be rising in the polls. It's a spiral. It's a downward spiral in which they have their own polls which justify their own coverage which causes less coverage and so on. It's very difficult impetus to reverse once you're going down in the polls.

Q.     The first time I saw Commoner's name in any poll was in August, at just less than one percent. By that time we were less than 90 days away from the election. How do you feel the national news media covered Commoner's candidacy versus that of Ed Clark and the Libertarian party? Clark, as you know, was on 50 ballots, Commoner was only, I believe, on about 30.

A.     How did they cover him? Well, I haven't done a line-by-line comparison.

Q.     Just your impression? Did you see any difference in how the national news media covered Clark versus Commoner?

A.     Yes. I did. I think the media was more puzzled by the libertarians. Libertarian philosophy makes an enormous distinction between domestic economic policy and foreign policy. Clark, launched ferocious attacks on the American role in Iran and was, I think, the only candidate including Commoner, to do a major attack on U.S.-Israeli relations. I don't know, I'd have to check, but certainly the libertarians were much more puzzling to the media which were a bit more uncertain how to treat them.

Q.      Clark, got four times as many votes but they were on the ballot in 20 more States.

A.      Yes, I think the libertarians pulled off a few tricks that the Commoner people didn't. I think that they were better organized than many others, particularly out in the West.

Q.      As far as raising money — and getting on the other 20 ballots — whereas the Citizens party wasn't able to organize?.

A.      I mean, there were some enormous problems in the Citizens party, as I recall, not getting on the ballot in Massachusetts. I remember feeling very depressed when I heard they hadn't gotten on that ballot.

Q.      The rules in Texas, where the citizen had to know his registration number to sign petitions, didn't help. I can't even remember my social security number.

A.      The fact of the matter is the libertarians did get on the ballot in 50 States and the Citizens party didn't, and that's to the credit of the Libertarian party. It shouldn't be forgotten however, that the Citizens party had a shorter time to prepare.

Q.      The libertarians had run four years...

A.      Yes, they'd been in the business longer. And they made a pretty good effort.

Q.      Do you see any way in the Orwellian year of 1984 for non-politicians like Barry Commoner or Ralph Nader to get the media to give them equal time on the issues versus, say, a Kennedy-Brown ticket or a Reagan-Bush ticket or a ticket headed by John Anderson?

A.      Well, there's nothing so easy as saying, "We must get media coverage." How do you get media coverage? You get media coverage to a certain extent, obviously, by discussing the issues. People might be likely to give your viewpoints time in one venue or another, whether it's documentaries, interviews, or it's adroit use of cable T.V.; there are various developments in which you're particularly interested. Ah, but you can't whistle up coverage without having a certain number of strings in your bow. One of them could be that the Citizens party has to become an impressive national force, by success in local elections, or lobbying — or in demonstrations. Obviously, coverage, to a certain extent, follows presence. No one can parachute themselves into 1984 and say, "I'm the alternative candidate! Give me coverage!" All you end up in is the ghetto: Those articles the press runs in the last week of the election campaign on the far left candidates, where they'll say, Here's the guy from the Workers World, and here's the guy from S.W.P. and so on. So, to a certain extent you've got to merit, and struggle for, the coverage and then in those crucial weeks when the campaigns are launched, you'll see a bit where you're going. But obviously, this depends a lot on your presence — learning the old rituals of New Hampshire, or whatever it is. Equally now, Brown is in a situation but I don't think Brown will be running in a year. Teddy Kennedy will always get coverage, that's a fact.

Q. The *Village Voice* endorsed Commoner for president. I remember there was quite a bit of criticism about how he stood on foreign policy and the economy. Could you touch on that for a moment.

A. Actually, it's a bit hard at this distance. I can't remember what the criticisms were specifically on the foreign policy side, or on the economy. I think maybe we felt that there was sometimes a certain paucity of depth in the ideas. I honestly don't want to go on the record with a statement regarding Commoner without reminding myself of the platform.

Q. When you flash back to the national convention in Cleveland where they put together this elaborate platform, do you feel maybe that was a little too general? Maybe he should have been a little more specific?

A. Oh, well, the conditions under which that platform was produced were so obviously pell-mell and being boiled out of different factions, that I don't think anything other than the document that finally emerged could possibly have emerged. It was a miracle, indeed, that whatever appeared, did appear. Obviously I might have specific areas of criticism; I might have a criticism on the Middle East; I might have a criticism on assessments of energy and on gasohol, but, no, I wouldn't be critical of the Cleveland platform.

Q.   It's purely hypothetical, but if in Cleveland, the party had nominated Nader instead of Commoner, do you think that Nader would have gotten many more votes and possibly could have really made a run at it?

A.   Look, I don't want us to get into the business of saying Nader is automatically more popular than Commoner. Obviously, they both have a lot of exposure.

Q.   Nader's a lot better known though — to the man in the street?

A.   Yes, I guess if you took a poll, maybe Nader's probably the best known consumer crusader in the country, and has been hard at it since 1964. But Commoner, of course, has been hard at admirable causes for even longer so I don't want definitely to say, but I guess it would be rational to say, that Nader would automatically recruit more votes than Commoner.

Q.   Will the "catch-22" go on forever, meaning: If you can't raise funds, you can't get exposure; which means the media ignores you; which means the public doesn't know you; which means you go back and teach at Queens College?

A.   Look at it this way. In 1984, John Anderson, or a person favored by John Anderson, is automatically on the ballot in 50 States and has, I think, about five or six million dollars to start off. This situation did not exist in 1980. It is possible not to go directly into the spiral which you've just invoked. Needless to say, any rational person will be pessimistic about the insertion of some really serious alternative challenge to the presidency. It would have to come out of the basis of a constituency. In the 1980 campaign, the constituency was split between the funds for Teddy, which negated any serious activity on the part of the Progressive Alliance, because it went into the Kennedy bid. It was disastrous, ultimately because the Kennedy bid was in vain. But I think it would be a great mistake to start speaking of The-Rich-Who-We-Are-Left-With are The-Rich-Who-Are-The-Two-Major-Candidates Syndrome. The obvious fact is that there is this pot of money — on the Anderson analogy of 1984 — which is something to be very seriously thought about. 1980 is followed by 1984 which is followed by 1988 and it's very easy to forget that, and to forget that consistency of effort. I mean, right now, there are obviously a lot of people talking on the labor side about how there should be a party of labor. These changes are slower than one thinks.

Q.     In your personal opinion as a journalist, do you feel that, on the issues, Anderson was saying things that Carter or Reagan weren't saying, or do you tend to think that David Garth packaged Anderson in such a way as to make him appear different? His image was different but, actually, on the issues, there weren't too many places he openly disagreed with either Carter and Reagan.

A.     No. I disagree with that last point. I think the interest in Anderson was pre-Garth. Garth tended to homogenize everything and send him off on routes of which I heartily disapproved, like the Middle Eastern trip. I thought it was ridiculous. And I think he ceased to be as interesting a candidate. I think this pre-Garth Anderson significantly differed from Carter and from Reagan in his attitudes. In the post-Afghanistan period his attitude on the cold war was courageous, I did more or less agree with most of his sentiments, his vigorous defense of SALT, and his refusal to be rendered hysterical by the Russian invasion of Afghanistan. I think at that point even his posture toward Pentagon spending was substantially different and I think it was at that moment that he was winning a lot of middle of the road votes from Americans with moderate attitude on the foreign policy questions. It was a substantial variation. It was the basis, incidentally, of my own and Jim Ridgeway's enthusiasm for him at various stages. We interviewed him in Boston, I think in February, 1980, and he made statements which we thought were courageous. Anderson also had things in his record which enabled people on the left to rush out and say he's the face of the Trilateral Commission. Just another face of big business. I don't think he is for a minute. George Wald and others said, he was put up by the trilateralists for some motive I can't fathom. I think Anderson — although I disagree with his energy policy and his gas rationing policy in the end — became a guy who said "I'm taking brave stands, look at me," as opposed to making the brave stands and then saying "Look at me!" The Anderson of the spring of 1980 was a very interesting candidate and I think the sadness was that he was badly mishandled. I think Garth got the whole thing completely wrong and Anderson himself got it wrong in the end.

Q.     Was it your impression that Anderson got a terrific amount of ink, versus other independents who had run in the past, and for that amount of ink, he garnered very few votes?

A.     Well, relative to ink, I suppose that's true.

Q.     In your opinion, between now and the '84 election, is there some way the media could get together and decide to have more open debates? For instance, at one point before Allard Lowenstein was shot, the rumors were that Kennedy was willing to debate Commoner on a platform with other people. Then that debate fell apart. Then at one point, Commoner challenged Anderson to a debate and Anderson said, "No, I won't debate you." At another point, Carter would not debate Anderson and Reagan on the same platform. Is there anything that can be done about all that?

A.     Debates will always be subject to the politician's tactical assessment at any given time. The media can create a position where it will appear embarrassing and shameful for a politician to skirt a debate. That conceivably could happen on one of the networks by 1984. But even so, I think basically in the end it is the calculation of the politician in question, and there is very little you can do to legislate a Kennedy-Commoner debate, or a Commoner-Anderson debate, unless they perceive it somewhat in their self-interest.

Q.     Can anything be done to change what I feel is really an overemphasis on polling? Polling that influences journalists and how they play the news?

A.     Like France not publishing the results of any polls a week before the election? That's just about the only way you can legislate it. Otherwise the polling will just continue on and on. It will get worse and worse. No, I don't think there's really anything you can do about that beyond just rendering publications of polls illegal at some point.

# "Talking To a Mule"
## by
### Barry Commoner
### Columbia Journalism Review,
### *January/February 1981, p.30-31*

On October 9, 1980 I delivered what I considered to be an important address to the Detroit Economic Club. It was important to me because, as the Citizens party candidate for president, I had been campaigning on a full time basis for nearly six months, yet I had attracted virtually no attention from the national news media. In Detroit I planned to lay out a detailed program for revitalization of the automobile industry based on a transition from gasoline to gasohol. Much of my speech was based on new research done at my environmental institute at Washington University. I believed, naively, that because I was speaking in a city whose life depends on the automobile industry — that because I was speaking before a prestigious forum, one that regularly draws such speakers as Henry Ford and Douglas Fraser — that because I was addressing national issues, the energy crisis and the economy — and that because I was reporting on new research — surely the news media would consider what I had to say important.

Imagine my shock when I discovered that my speech attracted almost no attention from the national press and that even the two local papers - the *Detroit News* and the *Detroit Free Press* — carried not a line on what I had said.

This was not an isolated incident. In six months of campaigning, hardly a word about the Citizens party had appeared in the national press or on the networks. We concluded that we had to reassess our campaign; a conclusion that, I suppose, should have been reached a month earlier when a television reporter said to me, "Dr. Commoner, are you a serious candidate or are you just running on the issues?"

Speaking out on the issues, as I had been doing on a daily basis throughout the campaign, clearly was inadequate to attract the kind of media attention we needed to get our message to the voters. Bill Zimmerman, my campaign manager, suggested that dealing with the national media was like talking to a mule; first you had to hit it over the head with a two-by-four to get its attention. With that thought in mind, he suggested a radio commercial starting out with a word that some newspapers quaintly refer to as a "barnyard epithet". Reluctantly, other party leaders and I agreed it had to be done. I say "reluctantly" not because of the use of the word. The dictionary defines it as "foolish, uninformed, and exaggerated talk." I think that accurately describes the empty campaign rhetoric offered in 1980 by Carter, Reagan, and Anderson. Our reluctance stemmed only from concern that we had to go to such lengths to capture the attention of the news media.

The result was spectacular. In two days the Citizens party received more news stories and broadcast time than it had received in its entire history. ABC's *World News Tonight* ran a segment on us; Walter Cronkite mentioned the commercial; *Good Morning America* and the *Today* show did pieces. Nearly every major newspaper in the country carried stories. But most interesting to me was a call my press secretary received from a reporter for the *Detroit Free Press*. That newspaper, which had carried not a word about my plan for revitalizing the auto industry, did run a front page story about the commercial. I think that is a sad commentary on the state of the profession.

For the first time, the *New York Times* called *us*. In addition to running a lengthy story the day after the commercial was aired, the *Times* simultaneously approved a long-standing request of Washington bureau reporter Philip Shabecoff that he be allowed to spend a few days covering me. The result was an excellent story about the substance of my campaign. Was the timing of approval for Shabecoff's request mere coincidence?

This and similar experiences during my campaign have emboldened me to offer some suggestions to the press on coverage of presidential elections. I believe journalists should reassess the way issues are covered. I think reporters should take a hard look at their relationships with the Democratic and Republican parties. And I think the news media should at least start listening to what nontraditional candidates are saying.

Every four years the media vows to take a serious attempt to cover the issues. This year, in some respects, they did better than in the past. The TV evening news shows featured series comparing the major candidates stands on some of the critical questions of the 1980s. And no less a pundit than the *Washington Post's* David Broder reported — somewhat breathlessly — that the *Des Moines Register* had been running a series of *front page* articles on the issues (my emphasis). Putting the "issues" on the evening news and front page was commendable, I suppose, but did it really serve the public?

Consider energy. I submit that by their own statements committing this country to continued dependence on nonrenewable energy, it was clear that neither Carter, Reagan, nor Anderson understood that issue. But by having the national debate on energy defined by the minute differences between their positions, we had no meaningful debate at all. It was like having a debate on religion in America with participation limited to Oral Roberts, Rex Humbard, and Jerry Falwell. Other issues as well — nuclear proliferation, environmental protection, and the one the Citizens party considered fundamental, corporate control of the economy — were not discussed by the major candidates and were therefore absent from the national debate. Is it any wonder so many Americans stayed home on election day?

In such a situation, in which the leading candidates' definition of the issues failed to produce adequate discussion, journalists had two options: they could have expanded the debate to other candidates or experts capable of addressing the issues fully and intelligently; or, at the least, they could have forced the major candidates to answer tough questions on the issues. They did neither. And so the media must take some responsibility for a campaign which, in a year that certainly did not lack critical issues, once again became an issueless popularity contest.

One of the roots of that problem, I believe, is the media's clear bias in favor of the two party system. The bias is pervasive and can be picked up from any major newspaper or network. When we announced formation of the Citizens party in August 1979, *Washington Star* political columnists Jack Germond and Jules Witcover wrote: "still another attack on the two party system" and criticized our efforts on the grounds that people involved with the Citizens party would be "unwilling to do the dirty work involved in getting into a position to influence the Republican and Democratic parties from within".

Well, what if you happen to believe that *influencing* the Republican and Democratic parties is not enough — that it is time for a new political force? We in the Citizens party believe the coalition parties which have to satisfy their conservative wings and rely on corporations for financing simply cannot address the fundamental issues of our time. Such parties are, in fact, part of the problem.

As a consequence of this bias, the immense resources devoted to reporting on what the major candidates and their running mates are doing, are far out of proportion to the news actually being made. I suppose I was most vexed during my lonely travels across the country when I saw George Bush — who had said publicly that his specific mission in the campaign was *not* to make any news — followed by a planeload of reporters and TV crews who dutifully reported every day that he had, in fact, made *no news*. I fail to understand how such allocation of valuable talent serves either the news media or the public.

I must acknowledge that during the campaign I was accorded many excellent interviews by local reporters that were given good play by newspapers and the electronic media alike. For that I was grateful, but unfortunately it is a truism that in a run for president it's the national news media that matters. A few reporters from major newspapers and networks occasionally were assigned to cover me, and some wrote excellent reports, but the majority were fascinated by the difficulties of running a campaign when you are not a major candidate. For example, an NBC news crew followed me for three days, including the day of my Detroit speech. Their report —

broadcast at 12:30 A.M., I might add — showed several scenes of me getting on and off commercial flights and being picked up at airports in small cars. The Detroit speech, which had been filmed, ended up on the cutting-room floor.

Let me acknowledge that I realize that the press has obligations in covering a presidential election that extend beyond simply reporting on the issues. It must report the news, and that means reporting on a daily basis what Carter and Reagan, as the leading candidates, did. However, I suggest that the press carried its obligations to an extreme by blocking out huge amounts of time or space to be filled whether or not the candidates made any news. It led to incredible trivilization. More Americans were aware that Nancy Reagan passed out candy and rolled oranges down the aisles of airplanes than knew that I was running for president.

I hope this doesn't sound like sour grapes from a losing candidate. I maintained from the outset that I had never expected to win, or even gain a significant percentage of the vote. I am simply frustrated that, after months of speaking out — I believe intelligently and informatively about the issues facing this country — my messages were not communicated to the electorate.

In the inevitable election post mortems, I believe the question most journalists should be asking themselves is: Did I, in 1980, adequately serve the majority of my readers, listeners, and viewers? The answer must, I think, take into account that fewer than half of all eligible Americans voted for Carter and Reagan combined. It is easy to write off the rest as apathetic, as unlikely ever to exercise their franchise. However, I happen to agree with Cornell Political Scientist Theodore J. Lowi, who views these Americans not as apathetic, but rather as *antipathetic*. They are opposed to the politics of the two party system, opposed to the only politics portrayed to them by the national news media. They might leave their homes and vote if the full range of available ideas and options were made known to them. Let's look at it another way, from a selfish journalistic perspective. Would a serious journalist want to cover another presidential election in which debate centers on such issues as: Did A say that B has the support of the Ku Klux Klan ? Is B the "nostalgia" candidate? Do we really want to reintroduce the Biblical interpretation of Genesis? Just as the Citizens party —and the libertarians for that matter — offered challenging new ideas in 1980, minority party candidates will be doing the same in years to come. Historically, the role of minority parties has been to bring forth such ideas. And, if such ideas are valid, the major parties eventually adopt them. Or, if the major parties are moribund — as was the case in the 1850s and may be the case in the 1980s — one of the minority parties achieves majority status. In either event, isn't reporting on the new ideas and identifying future political trends more exciting and significant journalism than what passed for political reporting this year?

I believe that this country is on the threshold of a major political realignment, and that the Citizens party will play an important role in it. But even if that doesn't happen, minority parties will continue to add zest to the political life of this nation. To journalists who might consider paying more attention to us, I'll make a pledge: We'll never promise *not to make news*. And I hope we won't have to resort to saying something outrageous just to get your attention.

# "Survey Shows Concern by Public for Press Fairness"

## by

### Dierdre Carmody, New York Times, October 25, 1981

Newspapers as well as television stations should be required by the government to present opposing views on important issues, according to a majority of the respondents to a national opinion survey on freedom of expression in the media.

This view was reiterated in several different ways by more than one thousand respondents representing a cross section of Americans questioned in connection with a report to be released tomorrow by the Public Agenda Foundation. The study's purpose was to identify how the public felt about freedom of expression in newspapers and broadcasting and to relay those attitudes back to leaders in the news media.

The most insistent theme in the report is the public's concern for fairness and the feeling of the respondents that the fairness standards of the news media, particularly newspapers, are not high enough. Most respondents to the survey said there should be laws requiring *fairness* by newspapers and television in the coverage of controversial issues and political candidates.

"The public's commitment to fairness transcends demographic and ideological categories," the report said. "Fairness is important to the least educated and the best educated, to liberals and conservatives and to people from all sections of the country."

For instance, the survey reported these findings:

- Of those questioned, 82 percent favored laws requiring that newspapers give each major party candidate the same amount of coverage; 81 percent said they thought television should give major party candidates the same amount of coverage.
- Seventy-three percent favored laws requiring newspapers to give opponents of a controversial policy as much coverage as proponents; 74 percent favored this for television.
- Sixty-three percent felt that there should be laws to require newspapers to cover candidates of major third parties.

The answers showed a confusion about existing regulations. Broadcasters are already subject to an equal time provision requiring that all legally qualified candidates for an office must be allowed the same amount of time. Broadcasters are also subject to the fairness doctrine, requiring that if one side of a controversial issue of public importance is presented, a reasonable opportunity must be afforded for the presentation of contrasting views.

Newspapers, however, are constitutionally protected from such legislation. The protection comes from the First Amendment, which says, "Congress shall make no law abridging the freedom of speech or of the press." The regulation of broadcasters has been justified under the First Amendment because the capacity of air waves is finite and someone must decide who will use them and who will not, a function of the F.C.C.

The survey also found a serious misunderstanding of public views by news media owners and executives.

"There is a tendency for communications professionals to misinterpret public calls for fairness as a demand for repression or direct censorship," Daniel Yankelovich, the pollster, president of the Public Agenda Foundation, wrote in the forward to the report. "This misconception has caused some leaders to discount public criticism of the media and to cast the public as an outsider with no legitimate stake of freedom of expression terms."

The report went on to state that this view had serious implications for freedom of expression in this country. Failure by news executives to acknowledge or respond to serious public concerns about lack of fairness in the media would erode public support for the First Amendment as we now know it, the report said.

"To ignore or misunderstand the public altogether, however, would be a very serious mistake indeed," Yankelovich wrote. "At the very least there is an obligation for leaders to explain to people why their position has been seriously considered and rejected."

The responses to the survey also showed a desire for the presentation of diverse points of view in newspapers and by radio and television stations. There was also a lack of support for news media autonomy, which the study warned should not be confused with a lack of concern for all aspects of freedom of expression.

The Public Agenda Foundation, a non-partisan organization, was founded in 1976 by Yankelovich and former Secretary of State Cyrus R. Vance. It conducts studies to discern public attitudes on issues such as inflation, energy and jobs. The studies have been intended to present public attitudes to national leaders who are involved in policy-making decisions.

William M. Ellinghaus is the group's president. Members of the policy reviews board include Derek C. Bok, president of Harvard University; John W. Gardner, head of *Common Cause*; Vernon E. Jordan Jr., president of the National Urban League, and Sol M. Linowitz, President Carter's representative for Middle East negotiations.

# An Interview With Tom Wicker
## Nationally Syndicated
New York Times *Columnist, 1981*
*Author of* On Press: A Top Reporter's Life in,
and Reflections on, American Journalism
*(Viking Press; 1978)*

*by*
*Jeffrey Gale*

Q.     Tom, perhaps you saw this quote in the last edition of *Life* magazine in 1980. They did some quotes from the campaign and there was one that said, "Are you a serious candidate, or are you just running on the issues?" A TV reporter asked that of Citizens party candidate Barry Commoner. In considering this quote I'd like to ask you; when you reflect back on the entire 1980 campaign, do you feel that this reflects on how the national media covered the entire presidential campaign, not just Barry Commoner's campaign, and what does this say to you? Could you give me your impression on this quote?

A.     Well, I don't know, the quote doesn't mean anything in particular to me; I don't think it's quite as silly as it sounds because election campaigns are fought out, of course, on many things other than issues. As a matter of fact, I think this is probably a fairly pertinent question to have put to Barry Commoner because I had discussions with him and I'm not sure he ever understood the extent to which issues are only one factor in the campaign.

Q.    Can you explain more of what you mean by that? In other words, do you feel that the national news media did a good job in covering the issues of the campaign — getting the candidates to really discuss the issues of the day?

A.    Of course not. They didn't even come close to anything like that. Candidates themselves don't discuss issues very much. I don't think it's the job of the news media to get candidates to talk about anything other than to answer the questions put to them. Whether or not the news media itself understands the national issues well enough is a matter of judgment. But I think we covered the campaign pretty well. Candidates don't talk very much about issues — they don't want to talk about issues — they want to talk about symbolic things and they want to project personalities and images and I think more and more the job of the news media in an election campaign — presidential campaigns particularly — is to cover how and why and to what purposes candidates project images because that's the major thing that's happening. You can say, if you want to, that the national press somehow ought to force candidates to sit down and discuss NATO and the nuclear bomb and so forth; but you can't do it and I'm not so sure that's the role of the press. So this whole question of covering the issues, I think is one of those questions that doesn't get to the reality of politics.

Q.    How do you feel the national news media covered Gene McCarthy's candidacy for the presidency in 1976 when he ran as an independent, versus the way they played John Anderson's campaign when *he* ran as an independent?

A.    They covered McCarthy almost not at all and the reason for that is two-fold, I think. By 1976, McCarthy — sadly enough, because I admire him — was a played-out figure in American politics. He was regarded almost as a Harold Stassen sort of candidate in '76. That's one reason that Anderson got a great deal more coverage. Anderson was a new face and a new face — an attractive new face — always gets more attention than an old face. The other thing is that Anderson ran in the Republican primary before becoming an independent and made quite a good showing and was discovered by American people as an articulate and attractive man and was thought for a good part of the campaign to have a pretty solid shot at it. He was taken more seriously on both counts, no question.

Q.     Do you feel that McCarthy's candidacy in '76 as dismal as it was, in a sense, paved the way for someone like Anderson to be able to make a fairly strong run as an independent in 1980, or do you feel that played a role at all?

A.     No, I don't think it did. I think if anything was a forerunner to John Anderson's campaign, and I don't mean ideologically, it could have been George Wallace's independent campaign. I've said it in regards to Gene McCarthy, to George Wallace and I've said it in regards to John Anderson, I think it's too bad that the system is so thoroughly stacked against the independent and third party candidates. I think part of the stacking against such candidates occurs because the press tends to assume that they are losers to begin with. A third party or an independent candidate is a minor candidate and therefore is perceived as a loser. Hence, you don't waste too much time with them. But I think one of the reasons that the press assumes that — and I'm not forgiving or bypassing the fact that the press does assume that — is the fact that the innate American political system is so stacked against third party and independent candidates, it's difficult to get on the ballot. Under the federal election system now, an Anderson or a Wallace can't get any campaign subsidy until after it's all over. The League of Women Voters set some kind of minimum qualifying standard to get into their debates and that left Anderson out of the last debate. And our whole election system in this country has been rigged to have two official parties and a two party system and I think that's too bad. I think it's not good for the parties — it's not good for the country — and there is nothing sacrosanct about a two party system — or either of the existing major parties.

Q.     The whole concept the Citizens party wanted to convey was to get away from 'imagery and personalities' and run only an issue-oriented campaign, as you know. However, this appeared to turn the media off. Do you think the media is so conditioned to covering personalities that only someone, say as famous as Ralph Nader perhaps, running for president in 1984 with Barry Commoner as his running mate, would stand a chance outside of the two party system?

A.     They wouldn't stand a chance either. Nader is not all that compelling a figure. You know, there's an assumption in all your questions that there is something really good and solid about running an issues-oriented campaign and anybody that doesn't recognize that is not covering politics in some correct manner and that anybody who follows the imagery of the symbolism of the campaign is not covering politics correctly. I think that's all wrong. If it is indeed true, as you've said in your question, that the Citizens party decided specifically to run an issues-oriented campaign only, then they decided to lose. I didn't make the world, and journalism didn't make the world. The voters are out there. They want to be interested. They want to know something about his wife, or her husband. They want to know something about his views on all kinds of things that are not, strictly speaking, issues. They've got a right to that. The press doesn't make them that way; they make the press that way.

But I think it's a two-part question. I think publications and broadcasters were influenced as to whom they would cover by the evidence of the polls. I don't particularly defend that, but it seems to me to be understandable. If some guy got two percent in the polls, you're not going to spend as much money. A network TV crew costs about two thousand dollars a day. You're not going to spend as much money on that two percent candidate as you would on Ronald Reagan who's running whatever he was in the polls at the time. On the other hand, however, your question: 'Did the national news media alter their coverage unless their polls came out right?' I think that's another baloney question. I don't understand an automatic assumption that somehow the press is so crooked that it would do things like that. I don't understand questions like that. I don't even care to answer it particularly.

Q.      Well, Tom, what went through my mind the first time I ever saw Barry Commoner's name show up in a poll, was in about August — about two or three months before the actual election. He showed up with less than one percent.

A.      People who didn't have him in the poll before were pretty solid in their assumptions.

Q.      How do you feel the national news media covered Commoner's candidacy, for instance, compared with that of Ed Clark and the Libertarian party? Do you see any difference?

A.      I don't have any comparative judgment, you know, like column inches or numbers or pictures or anything like that; but my impression, looking back on it, is that Clark got marginally more press than Commoner and I would guess that if that is correct at all it was probably because Clark generated more funds for television advertising and so forth. I think Clark was, in that sense, more of a presence in the campaign and, in fact, finally got more votes, did he not?

Q.      He got, I believe, four times as many votes. He was on fifty ballots, Commoner was on thirty, but of course, Clark and the libertarians, had run in the past. The Citizens party had never run in the past.

A.      That's right. And I think those marginal differences gave him marginally more press coverage, that's my impression.

Q.      Do you see any way in the year of 1984 for a non-politician like Barry Commoner, Ralph Nader, or anyone else to get the media to give them equal time on the issues versus say a Teddy Kennedy-Jerry Brown ticket or a Ronald Reagan-George Bush ticket or a ticket headed by John Anderson?

A.      No. You will not get equal time in the press, if you're perceived as a straight-out loser, if you're perceived as not having any chance. You say non-politician. I don't know what that means. Anybody who runs for office, to me, is a politician. But let us just suppose in this past year that Walter Cronkite had run for office as an independent. I guarantee you he would have received a lot more coverage than Barry Commoner got, probably a lot more votes, too.

Q.     Do you think Ralph Nader would, Tom?

A.     No. I don't think Ralph Nader is that kind of figure myself, although I have no doubt he would make a good showing. The main thing in this country, if you are going to mount a campaign strictly on what you perceive to be the issues — and that's a subjective judgment — and insisting that you are right on the issues, and you're not going to talk about anything but the percentage of oil imports and that sort of thing, and if you're running outside the major party apparatus, I tell you that's a loser and it's going to be perceived that way. Now, if you can get Walter Cronkite to head your ticket — or if you could get...I'm sure we could sit here and think of five other public figures who'd automatically get that kind of attention — that would be one thing. But even a man as electorally respected and as well known in his particular circles as Barry Commoner, is not going to get it on that basis.

Q.     Do you feel that the "catch-22" will go on forever? Meaning, if you can't raise funds, you can't get exposure, which means the media ignores you, which means the public doesn't know you, which means you go back and teach at Queens College?

A.     I wouldn't quite label that a "catch-22." There's a "catch-22," I think, for established political figures with political background (like John Anderson was this past year, or like George Wallace was) to run independent or third party campaigns. No question of that. As I said earlier, the system is stacked against it. But even if it weren't, and even if we had a different system, I still think that the Commoner ticket last year wouldn't have gotten much attention and couldn't have gotten any votes because it just wasn't the kind of campaign that is going to catch the attention of the American public. Now, it will be asked whether it would catch the attention of the American public if the press would pay some attention. But you see, there is the circular thing here; the press is not, as you have suggested with some of your questions, some monolithic kind of machine that sits up here and registers preferences, or does this or does that because it wants to. The press is constantly trying to gauge the public and they may be right or they may be wrong, but they gauged that the public didn't care about the Barry Commoner campaign, by and large, and that's why they didn't cover it. Now, I don't question that if they had elected to cover it, it would have done better at the polls — not much better — but better. But on the other hand, why would editors have elected to cover it? It wasn't making that much of an impression. I don't say it won't the next time around, if they keep that party in beat, — if they keep working at it. The libertarians, I think have, in about three elections, gained very substantially and I think they will do better next time.

Q.  During the middle of the campaign at one point I talked to Irvin Horowitz, your assistant national news editor, and asked about the coverage of Commoner. He said that the *Times* had run the page one, one-on-one interviews,(Bob Scheer did the same thing for the *L.A. Times*). I then asked, 'What about the decision that had been made at the *Times* not to do anything until both the Democratic and Republican National Conventions were over?' I'd like to ask you whether you knew — as associate editor of the paper — about the inner workings of the *New York Times* and how much coverage the *New York Times* decided to give Barry Commoner versus Clark or Anderson or anyone else?

A.  I don't know, because I don't have anything to do with the news coverage. I write my column and that's it. The associate editor doesn't believe that I have anything to do with the news department. But I could guess that it is not a question of deciding how much coverage to give. That sounds more like some cosmic decision to decide what we're not going to cover or what we are. *It's that nobody ever saw in the Commoner campaign anything of much news value.* I'm giving you a journalist's point of view here and I'm sure I'm wrong on some of these things, but I just think it's too easy for political candidates and parties, who have not mounted an effective campaign, to turn around and blame it on the press. American political history will show you, from its very start, that a campaign which set out to focus on issues and nothing but issues and on what the candidate thinks of the issues, is a loser. That campaign was a loser for just that reason.

Q.  George Wallace, never made that mistake. George Wallace made a much better show than Barry Commoner. If I'm not mistaken, John Anderson got as much national media coverage or more than Wallace did in that campaign. Why do you think that Anderson got so few votes and so much national media attention?

A.      Anderson and Wallace both started with something like 20-odd percent of the vote. I think Wallace had an almost fixed constituency, and he could sink as a national figure down to the level of his fixed constituency and then wouldn't sink anymore because they were going to vote for him no matter what. Anderson, I don't think, ever had any such constituencies. He had basically a constituency made up of some people who liked him and a lot of people who didn't like either Reagan or Carter. As the election got near and it became clear that Anderson was not going to win, those people who just were voting for him because they didn't like the other guys, went back to whichever of the other guys they preferred. I think Wallace finally got about fourteen percent of the vote did he not? And I think that pretty accurately reflected Wallace's absolute bedrock constituency. He would have gotten 14 percent of the vote, you know, by throwing his hat in the air and doing nothing else.

Q.      Do you really think that Anderson, when you examine the speeches that he made and how he stood on the issues, was saying very much that Carter or Reagan wasn't saying?

A.      No. But I've tried to explain to you and you keep coming back to it. These elections are not fought out on issues in that sense. No, I don't maintain at all that Anderson said any more about the issues than anybody else, probably less than some of the others.

Q.      Do you think that in any way David Garth was able to shape the latter parts, the key parts, of the campaign to make it appear to the media and to the public that Anderson was really saying something different on the issues than Carter and Reagan, when perhaps he really wasn't? In other words, his image was different but what he was really saying wasn't.

A.      I don't think Garth had any success with that. Just look at the downward trail of the Anderson vote.

Q.      The first time I ever heard that Barry Commoner was being considered to run, was right after Donahue had him on. Allegedly hundreds of people called in and said, "Would you consider helping found a new political party and maybe Ralph Nader would run for president and you could run with him, and you'll go into the New Hampshire primary together?" Do you think Barry Commoner was perceived by the media from the very beginning as being a one-issue candidate, anti-nuke, and in that sense like Wallace, was a one-issue candidate? Or do you think that the media portrayed Barry Commoner as being a multi-issue candidate who had more to offer than to just stand up and say "I've been against nuclear plants since 1947?"

A.     I don't think the media portrayed him in any way, shape or form. I've never thought that he was only an anti-nuke candidate and I think that the press coverage he got was sketchy enough that he was not portrayed in any fashion except as a loser — as a minor candidate.

Q.     In other words, Tom, the big anti-nuke rally in New York allegedly drew about 230,000 people — that's how many votes Barry Commoner got when he ran for president of the United States.

A.     Well, you may think he was just a single-issue candidate, I never thought of him that way.

Q.     I never felt you did, Tom. What I'm getting at is — I was wondering on a national scope how you feel they portrayed his candidacy?

A.     Well, I'm trying to say, I don't think they did portray his candidacy. People may have read that Commoner is a one-issue candidate, but I think basically the press gave its minimum coverage to what the man said and did, maybe less than minimum and the total portrayal that came through was not of a one-issue candidate or anti-nuke, or left-winger, or right-winger, or anything of that sort, but of a minor candidate who was going to lose.

Q.     And, of course, the alternative media like *Rolling Stone*, *Mother Jones* and the *Village Voice* seemed to give him a whole lot of attention. Bill Moyers had him on for an hour on *Bill Moyers' Journal*, but when you look at what we might call the establishment media, I rarely saw his face on television. He was never on *Issues and Answers*; he was never on *Face the Nation.*

A.     That's right, because those people are interested in what they consider to be the winners, or people who are likely to win. I know the cyclical argument you make that if they would only have him on, then he would be a person who might win. Since they don't have him on, he is a person who won't win. But what are you going to do if you are a newspaper or television editor and you've got to make judgments all the time about these things? And I must say, I don't consider at any point, from the beginning to end, that the Commoner Citizens party campaign had a remote chance to win or carry any states or anything of the sort. Now that's not to say that he couldn't, by astute political work and advertising and all sorts of other aspects of American politics, become a force in American politics; but they weren't the last time around and I don't think it was lack of media attention that was their downfall. It was the nature of their campaign that meant they were not going to get any media coverage.

# An Interview With Barry Commoner
## "The Solar Answer"
### Suburbia Today,
### Gannett Westchester Rockland Newspaper
### May 10, 1981 p. 7-9

### by
### Loren Stell

A biologist, Commoner has long been an environmentalist leader, having started his Center for the Biology of Natural Systems in 1966 at St. Louis' Washington University. His book, *The Closing Circle*, sums up many of the findings of his early work.

The environmental studies led to Commoner's interest in the energy crisis, which resulted in his most recent volume, *The Politics of Energy*.

Commoner didn't get much coverage in last year's campaign until he used a barnyard term in a radio spot to criticize Reagan and Carter Policies. That was too bad, because his views are startling in their common sense simplicity.

Working out of his center, now based at Queens College, Commoner plans to apply the "solar transition" to a block of row houses. He will first install a cogenerator — an engine that can provide space heat while making electricity — and later add solar panels and photovoltaic cells.

The implications of the project are broad. If it is practical on a wide scale, the nation would burn less of its scarcest fuels. In addition, each American family would gain far more control over its energy production and costs. Commoner's ideas could, in short, truly return power to the people, as he explains.

Before deciding to run for president last year, Dr. Barry Commoner took a long survey of the political ticket. He saw Jimmy Carter wandering, lost. He feared the havoc of Ronald Reagan's budget machete and military spending. Only a new party, he believed, could begin the natural process that would return the nation to its place in the sun.

That he captured less than one percent of the vote doesn't bother him. He says his campaign firmly established the Citizens party, dedicated to the proposition that Americans don't have to be impoverished by the high cost of energy or by the mistakes of reckless corporations chasing profits.

As Reagan arrived in Washington, the energetic Commoner, now 63, bobbed up in his native New York City, where he has begun to offer new prescriptions for our energy ills.

The engine for change is the sun, now the only feasible long-term hope, according to Commoner. He says the nation and the world must make the "solar transition" to renewable fuels. He is opposed to the alternative offered by nuclear proponents: breeder reactors that are supposed to make more nuclear fuel than they burn. Such reactors, Commoner says, are too expensive, too complicated, too unreliable and too dangerous.

Q.     Dr. Commoner, can New York really cut down its appetite for energy?

A.     Absolutely. In Queens, we are introducing energy-saving and solar processes into areas where poor people live, because the poor suffer most in the energy crisis. Up to now, steps taken to introduce money-saving solar energy have been directed at people who can afford a $25,000 increase on their mortgage. But thousands of lower-income families have an option they haven't yet heard about.

Q.     To make the solar transition?

A.     Right. Cogeneration — the production of electricity without throwing away the heat made in the process — is the key to an energy-efficient system.

People can form small energy cooperatives out of a group of row houses. In a row house, you've got a group of houses with just one wall between their basements. Our idea is to put a cogenerator in one building that would produce electricity and heat for the entire row house block, delivered by a single pipe driven through the interconnecting walls.

Once that's set up, the savings start immediately; because, in generating your own electricity, you are also producing free heat. *Then* you can begin to introduce solar savings in three different ways: by putting heat collectors on the roof and adding it into the circulating hot water from the cogenerator; installing photovoltaic cells when the price comes down; and finally by the substitution of methane produced from garbage or sewage for the natural gas burned in your cogenerators.

Q.   Are these cogenerators just converted auto engines?

A.   Yes, four-cylinder Fiat engines, which have been converted to burn natural gas instead of gasoline. In Europe they're very popular and are often used banded together. There is no reason why such units couldn't be made in the U.S. You would have to design the whole thing, but it's not terribly complicated.

Q.   Why did you pick row houses, rather than high-rises?

A.   The practicality of cogeneration in high-rise apartment buildings is known in Europe and here. Several huge complexes in Brooklyn and Queens already have cogeneration units. But you have more difficulty introducing solar energy, in high rises, because tall buildings have relatively little roof space.

There are millions of row houses up and down the East Coast that could take advantage of cogeneration and solar energy. What we're going to do is develop an optimal energy system — and also a way of evaluating any given set of row houses with respect to their structure — so that any metropolitan home-owner group can compute how big a cogenerator has to be, what the relative advantages would be, what value solar heaters would add, and so on...

Row houses are ideal in the city. In the suburbs, one-family houses in small neighborhoods could be connected by pipes in ditches. Although no one I know of in the suburbs has built such a district-heating system, neighborhood cogeneration will eventually be economical too, especially because suburban houses have more roof area available for solar devices.

Q.    If everyone begins producing his own electricity, how would that affect the utility companies?

A.    Wall street is no longer looking at utilities as a good investment and very soon neighborhoods might start out competing them in producing cheap energy. In a solar transition, of course, utilities everywhere are going to be in trouble. It is very unlikely that they can maintain a centralized power grid as a private enterprise. They probably should all go into public ownership.

Q.    Until that happens, how would your row house cogenerators hook up to the utility system?

A.    The mathematics will have to be worked out. You could keep the size of the row house cogenerator down, and when there is a peak demand for the use of electricity — in the middle of the summer — you may buy from Con Edison.

On the other hand, you may choose to have a cogenerator big enough so that you could always meet your peak demand. Then you're bound to have extra electricity in the winter. So you'd sell it. Con Edison wouldn't like that, but they'd have to buy it. There are rules about that now.

Q.    What other projects are underway at the center?

A.    We have come up with a method of analyzing urine to determine whether a person has been exposed to carcinogens. Here we hope to test children's urine — since they are not industrially exposed and not smoking — in order to get a picture of the distribution of carcinogens in the general environment.

We plan to test kids in the city and the suburbs, particularly northern New Jersey where there are heavy levels of pollution.

Also, we are trying to research whether it's possible to pump up the sludge that's been dumped offshore all these years in the New York bight and convert it into methane.

Q.    Aren't you going to have to sign up a billionaire to help you get these projects off the ground?

A.      It's going to be very hard, because the research money we have been using has largely depended on the federal government. Now Reagan has decided that the Department of Energy should be reduced to exploring nuclear power — precisely the wrong thing to do.

Q.      Would you say that you hope to make New York self-reliant?

A.      Certainly not. It's out of the question. Self-reliance is a trap in some ways. When I testified before Congress, I calculated that there just isn't enough solar area in Manhattan to support the people who live there. New York will always have to depend on imported energy.

Q.      That might take a whole Middle East oil field.

A.      Not necessarily. The imported energy should be solar energy. The important thing to do now in New York and other big cities is to set up systems that will readily accept imported solar energy. That's why natural gas is so important. Because the natural gas pipe system can also accept methane gas from biomass, such as farmer's compost or garbage. There is a plan to pipe methane from the Pelham Bay Park landfill to Co-Op City, for instance. This is a form of renewable solar energy. Our studies have shown that the most efficient and economical way to cogenerate electricity and heat locally is with methane gas.

Q.      Why not generate electricity centrally as we do now?

A.      The main reason is that the most energetic way to transmit energy — that is, with the least loss — is by piping gas. Transmitting electricity over distance is very wasteful. It has to overcome resistance in the lines. More, when you conduct electricity from a central power plant, you are producing an awful lot of heat at one place and it's difficult to get enough people to live around a plant to make efficient use of that heat. Beyond that, the biggest expense is the amount of capital needed for central plants, especially for nuclear-produced electricity.

Q.      Not a lot of people are heading to Three Mile Island.

A.      That's right. When people learn that decentralized production of electricity — through cogenerators — makes sense, then the need for methane and natural gas becomes obvious.

With people living close together, you have to have a fuel for their cogenerators that won't pollute. And natural gas and methane does not pollute — back to the row house project.

What we are doing makes sense today simply based on the economics of cogeneration. Eventually, my idea is that surplus methane produced from boimass plants above ground could be pumped the other way back to underground into natural gas tanks.

Q.     You've come a long way from where you started — with air, earth and water — to this over-riding concern about energy.

A.     Our environmental research led us to energy. The pollution problems came about because of faults in our production system — the way in which we produce cars, fabrics and food. In many ways, energy is the most crucial element in redesigning our system of production. Without energy, no production takes place. If you reduce my concern to one central theme, it's not pollution *or* energy. It's reorganizing the system of production. That explains why I went into politics. We will need profound political reorganization to confront the problems of energy and pollution.

Q.     Besides talking about corporate mismanagement due to the goals of simply making profits, you've written that pollution — and the huge debt it's incurred — also makes political reorganization a necessity.

A.     Absolutely. Take the business of toxic wastes. There are at least five thousand "Love Canals" all over the country. How large a problem they present can be seen from the super fund Congress voted to begin the cleanup. A lot of taxpayers' money has been unnecessarily wasted. How did this happen?

Basically, it happened because of the development of the petrochemical industry after World War II, which proceeded to put a burden on the environment. It was cheaper for the companies to just dump waste, rather than to detoxify the poisons. But cleaning it up now is a lot more expensive than to have prevented it in the first place.

The question has never been asked, when these decisions are made, "Is this going to be good for the people of the country?"

No, the essential decision is made by a corporation asking only one question, "Is this good for our corporation, for our profits? And if it is, we'll do it." Then *later* we discover whether it is good or bad for the country.

In the *Closing Circle* I wrote that a series of decisions made by the auto companies, the utilities and the petrochemical industry — decisions good for short-term profits — were bad and unprofitable for the country. This raises the basic issue: How do we prevent such corporate short-sightedness?

Q.  Was this part of your concern when you were campaigning for the Citizens party?

A.  Right. We are heading for very serious economic problems. We've got an auto industry that is deteriorating, we've got a subway system in New York — and mass transit all over — that's in bad shape; we've got inflation and unemployment. Clearly, we have to rebuild the economy.

The energy crisis leads to various opportunities to rebuild in a much more efficient way. For example, we could have our auto system on alcohol, as in Brazil, which is moving into the total alcohol fuel. The Ford factory there is building one hundred percent alcohol-fueled cars. People are buying them as fast as they can build them. Imagine if we did that here?

Q.  Then the energy crisis may actually lead to an economic upswing?

A.  Perhaps. But it's going to take major capital investment, and I don't see any way of getting the capital unless we cut drastically the capital we're wasting in military production.

It's no accident that the highest rate of inflation in any industrialized country is in Israel, because the Israeli economy has been so heavily turned toward the military. Among the large countries, the U.S. has the highest rate of inflation. And, of the large countries, the U.S., has the highest percentage of its budget going into the military.

At the other end of the scale are Japan and West Germany. They're in great economic shape because they cleverly lost World War II and for many years were held back by the treaties from investing in the military. This simple fact — that big increases in unproductive military spending pushes inflation higher — is being ignored totally by the Reagan administration.

Q.     How did your campaign audiences respond when you spoke this way?

A.     A lot of them would say at first: "My God, the Russians will overrun us if you take this stance. The huge military expense is justified, because we are in danger."

I'd tell them another way to look at it is to remember what we were told by the administration at the time of the Vietnam War: that we *had* to get involved because of this threat to the U.S. and because of Soviet and Chinese expansion. We listened, got involved and lost. And even though we lost, we haven't been threatened. If it's true, as any objective military expert will tell you, that the government in Vietnam is not a threat to the U.S. it means the entire tragedy — the huge expenditure in Vietnam — served no purpose relative to our security.

Q.     Estimates range as high as two hundred billion dollars, I believe.

A.     And thousands of lives. And, in some ways even more importantly, Vietnam destroyed the credibility of the government so much so, that the people have now elected a president who is basically an anarchist.

Q.     How are you defining anarchist?

A.     Reagan, I consider to be, in a sense, an anarchist. He tells us the big problem is the government. That's what anarchy is about. Anarchists claim that if you do away with the government, everything will be all right. And, as you might imagine, I consider that bad, because government allows us to improve civilized life.

Q.     Out in the hustings, when you were trying to get elected...

A.     I wasn't trying to get elected. That was not my mandate or intention. We were organizing a party... And the Citizens party is established now. Of course, the election was very strange in many ways. Nationally we received .27 percent of the vote. You say that's very little. But it's not an accurate measure of our constituency.

Wherever we had a local candidate, the vote was enormously higher. In Missouri, where we had write-in campaigns, two local candidates ran. One got 10 percent of the vote and the other 19 percent. This makes me believe that our true constituency is about 10 percent.

Q. What are some of the issues that the Citizens party will be keeping alive?

A. Well, expenditures on public enterprises — water, sanitation and garbage — have been neglected. The propaganda against public expenditures has had a disastrous effect on the quality of these systems and therefore on the quality of life. There is no way we're going to have a decent standard of living without paying attention to these things. For example, maintenance and development of the whole New York City water supply has been neglected, as has been the mass-transit system.

Q. Have you a vision of what a solar New York would be like?

A. One of the things that would be immediately apparent would be the neighborhoodness of the city. Clearly what would be happening would be the establishment of local cooperatives. They would begin initially around the business of producing energy and you can see how the thing would spin out.

You might have a row house cooperative or a block association covering one block or 10 square blocks. An issue in the neighborhood newsletter might be, since there would likely be an excess of energy generated at the co-op power station, "Hey, why don't we buy some electric cars for the neighborhood that all members could use to go shopping?" The batteries would sop up the extra electricity and members would be provided with a convenient service.

The cars and the generating plant would provide jobs for local people. And out of that might come the notion of also buying an electric truck to go outside the city to a farmers' cooperative to pick up food where it's freshest.

Eventually perhaps, some food co-ops might link up with the energy co-ops. These new associations of consumers would invade the territory which is now thought to be the province of the utilities and the supermarkets. Maybe a few windmills would whirl and garbage collection would gain in status — it would be an important resource for methane for cogenerators.

Q.     Is it possible, using some of the logic in the *Closing Circle*, to say our government had to learn to close it's own circle?

A.     I don't usually equate biological and social issues. Science deals with molecules, not people...

What I was talking about in the book was the origin of life. The way in which it happened was that we had organic matter laid down chemically on the surface of the earth. The first living things arose as users of the organic matter. That's where they got their energy. And if nothing else had happened, life would very soon have gone right down the drain — using up all the earth's organic matter.

But photosynthesis arose, a natural means of constantly re-creating organic matter, as in plants, through solar energy — thus closing the circle. If it weren't for that closed circle, we wouldn't be here today. Our system of production is now dealing with our resources in this unilateral way — and failing to recognize the need to fit into this balanced system. We now have to restore the integrity of the system.

Q.     I still wonder if you can't extend your metaphor? If the profit motive can be seen as a linear kind of phenomenon — unwittingly using up the earth's resources without replacing them — then shouldn't enlightened government "close the circle" and create a kind of "human photosynthesis?"

A.     It's not inevitable that we will succeed as nature does. But I would agree; what we must have is a government that recognizes the need for concerted social action as a way of sustaining individual human lives.

# An Interview with Jack Nelson
## Washington Bureau Chief of the
## Los Angeles Times; 1982
## Weekly Panelist,
## "Washington Week in Review" (PBS)

### by
### Jeffrey Gale

Q.    How do you feel the national news media did overall in covering the 1980 presidential election versus the 1976 election?

A.    Well, it's kind of hard to compare the two, but I would guess that they did a little better. The reason I say that, is because newspapers looked at the '76 coverage — I know the *L.A. Times* did — and we decided we had not gotten into the coverage early enough to see where all the candidates were, what they were doing and for what they stood. I think we got into it earlier in 1980. Also in 1980, we did more I believe, of not following everything that was said day-to-day by all of the candidates, but kind of stepped back and tried to do a piece, say, at the end of the week, on what had happened every day that week and then put it into more of a comprehensive story.

Q.    Can we explore this a little? For example, was a meeting set up with Bill Thomas, or with Bob Scheer, yourself, George Skelton, a series of people, where perhaps you said, 'Okay, here's how we covered 1976 when Eugene McCarthy, was a candidate. Now we have 1980 and it looks like a guy named Clark is going to be running and a guy named Commoner may run, and Anderson ...' In other words, did you really sit down at a round table and have a discussion?

A.      No. We had several meetings in the Washington bureau among people covering the campaign. In addition to that, there were a lot of telephone conversations back and forth if I remember correctly — and Skelton can tell you this better than I — there was at least one meeting in Los Angeles where Dennis Britton, the national news editor, Dick Cooper the news editor of the Washington bureau, myself and several others sat down and discussed what we would be doing in the campaign in 1980.

Q.      Was the procedure in '76 and in '80 the same, where they assigned one journalist to cover one particular candidate, as perhaps you were assigned to cover Carter? How did that work?

A.      Individual reporters were assigned to cover candidates, but there was a lot of swapping. I mean, someone might cover Carter for one week, and the next week, I might cover Reagan. There was a lot of swapping around. Early on, certain people were assigned to Anderson and, of course, when he dropped out, those people had nothing to do in the campaign.

Q.      Was that different than the coverage in '76 — the way those assignments went? Was there anything specifically different at the *L.A. Times*?

A.      No, I don't think, in connection with the assigning to particular candidates, it was different. I think it was very much the same.

Q.      How do you feel the national news media covered Gene McCarthy's candidacy for the presidency in 1976 when he ran as an independent versus the way they played John Anderson's campaign when *he* ran as an independent?

A.      Well, as I remember it, the McCarthy candidacy was not covered as thoroughly as the Anderson candidacy simply because Anderson was considered, in the beginning at least, to have had more of a chance to pull some sort of an upset. So in my opinion, Anderson got much more coverage.

Q.    In other words, because Anderson ran in the primaries as a republican and showed up better in the polls, a decision was made to give him more play than someone like McCarthy, who, as I recall, didn't run in the primaries in '76?

A.    That's right. And I think probably another factor was that John Anderson had a lot of contacts, people in the Washington press corps, which he used to good advantage by giving them priority to what he was doing. He was a very articulate candidate and people did think that even if he didn't win, he could make the difference between whether Reagan or Carter won.

Q.    The whole concept the Citizens party wanted to convey, as far as I know, was to get away from imagery and personalities and run only an issues-oriented campaign. As you know, however, this appeared to turn the media off. Do you think that the national news media is so conditioned to covering the personalities of the candidates that only someone as famous as, say, Ralph Nader, running for president in 1984, with Barry Commoner as his running mate, would stand any kind of a chance outside of the two party system?

A.    I'm not sure that Ralph Nader would stand a chance either. But I think what happens is that, particularly with television coverage of campaigns, personalities are more important than ever because television needs the personalities. Let's face it, television has a lot to do with what newspapers cover, even though you can say that the *Washington Post* and the *New York Times* and perhaps the *Los Angeles Times* may sometimes help set the agenda on what the networks are covering. Television helps set the agenda on what everybody is covering because, if they lead their evening newscasts with big stories on Anderson, Carter or Reagan, the newspapers are almost inclined to follow suit in the media the next day.

Q.    Do you feel that the establishment media, with large corporate holdings on a national level, made an early decision to play down its coverage of the anti-corporate Citizens party and Dr. Commoner, who up to that point, was a non-politician?

A.    No. Because I don't think there are any corporate decisions made in political coverage. I've never heard of any. And I know there are not any as far as the *Los Angeles Times* is concerned. I worked on the *Atlanta Constitution* and I worked on the *Savannah Morning News*. I worked on the Biloxi, Mississippi, *Daily Herald* and I've never heard of a corporate decision in connection with any political campaign, local, state or national. I just don't think that happens. I'm not saying that *no* newspaper has ever had the corporate side of the paper influence it in political coverage, it may have. All I'm saying is that, in my own career as a reporter (which is 32 years) I've never heard or seen corporate interests have any sort of role in what you did or didn't cover.

Q.     To what extent do you feel major news organizations were influenced by the polls in how much coverage to give the candidate and did some even go so far as to justify the amount of coverage given to make their own in-house polls seem accurate? In other words, back in the days when you started out, there was a Roper Poll, there was a Gallup Poll, now it seems like every major news organization and every candidate has its own pollster.

A.     I don't think they use their own polls to try to justify their coverage or to try to show that what they have seen in the other polls is right. I know it's true — if you were to see a candidate suddenly shoot up in the polls from eight percent to 20 percent, he would get more attention from the news media. There is no question about it, and it would be strictly on the basis of whether he looks like a very serious candidate, whether he may have a chance to win. You can look back at the George Wallace candidacy, particularly George Wallace in 1968 when he shot up in the polls. I mean he got tremendous coverage and it was not just because he was George Wallace, the demagogue who was well known for his stand on segregation and so forth, but because he went way up in the polls. He got tremendous attention.

Q.     How do you feel the national news media covered Commoner's candidacy versus that of Ed Clark and the Libertarian party as you look back at the whole thing now?

A.     Well, they gave Ed Clark and the Libertarian party more cov-

erage than they did Commoner but I think it was because Ed
Clark and the Libertarian party made more headway, had more
money and were more visible from their ads. I think that had a
lot to do with it.

Q.     In other words, the fact that the libertarians had run for years
earlier and the libertarians were on all 50 ballots whereas
Commoner and the Citizens party only were on 30 ballots made
a big difference?

A.     Exactly. Not only were they on all 50 ballots, but they
apparently had more resources: they were on the air, ran their
own ads and so forth and they were invited, apparently, on more
public forums than Commoner. Again, it looked like more of a
factor, maybe not a chance to win, but more of a factor into what
might happen.

Q.     Do you see any way in the year 1984 for non-politicians like
Barry Commoner or, a Ralph Nader, to get the media to give them
equal time on the issues versus a Kennedy/Brown ticket or a
Reagan/Bush ticket or a ticket headed by John Anderson?

A.     No, I would doubt seriously that anybody who is not known,
who has not gone up in the polls, who is not seen as a serious
candidate or seems to have a serious chance to win, would get
the kind of coverage you're talking about.

Q.     In the very beginning, I recall some of the founders of the
Citizens party saying that what they intended to do was to have
Ralph Nader and Barry Commoner go into New Hampshire long
before the New Hampshire primary and get involved in that way.
It turned out that they didn't have the funding and they decided
to pull back and not do it. They waited until April and had a
convention in Cleveland. So your feeling is that for anyone to get
elected in 1984, be they politician or not, they would have to go
through the primary system?

A.     Yes, I would say they'd have to go through the primary
system. They have to do something to establish that they have a
serious chance of winning and the primary system seems to be
the only way to do that.

Q.     Will the "catch-22" as I call it, go on forever? Meaning, if you
can't raise funds, you can't get exposure, which means the media

ignores you, which means the public doesn't know you, which means that if you're like Barry Commoner you go back and teach at Queens College?

A.     I think that's very accurate. I mean that's really true. You are caught in a no win situation because you don't have the money and you can't get the exposure. You don't get the attention, but you've got to do something to show you have that serious chance, whether it's getting into the New Hampshire primary early and spending all your resources there and making a credible showing, or whether it's doing something else in one of the early primaries. But you've got to do it or the media isn't going to pay any attention to you.

Q.     I'm going to ask you a couple of questions that get a little more specific and I'll give you some of the background. At the *Los Angeles Times*, the editors assigned Robert Scheer to do front page one-on-one interviews with all candidates during the primaries, but would not allow him to interview Barry Commoner until after the primaries. They then buried the interview inside the paper and cut it very short. *Los Angeles Times* media critic David Shaw told me, "Anderson got far more ink in our paper than he deserved versus Commoner who was really the alternative candidate in the election on the issues, not Anderson." Kenneth Reich, political writer for the *Times,* told me, "If it were up to me, I would never assign Bob Scheer to do an in-depth, one-on-one interview with Barry Commoner." Reich covered the Anderson campaign, or at least part of it in California, but the *Times* did not have a by-line reporter cover the Citizens party convention in Cleveland in April of 1980 when Commoner was nominated. They waited until late summer to assign Lee May of the Washington bureau to do a brief news story involving Commoner's candidacy. It was the first by-line piece by an *L.A. Times* staffer on the Citizens party up to that point, yet they covered Anderson almost on a daily basis. Scheer was originally going to consider interviewing Commoner earlier in the campaign, but like the *New York Times*, waited until after the democratic and republican conventions were over before paying any attention to him. This I propose was all done by design. The media, as Ben Bradlee of the *Washington Post* said in a taped interview with me, made a conscience decision that because they felt Commoner could not raise enough funds to get on all 50 ballots like Anderson did, he could not win the election. And thus, no matter how important his statement of the issues appeared to be, he and Ed Clark of the Libertarian party, who was on all 50 ballots, was not in the horse race. Bradlee and other editors did not see it as their duty to assign journalists to a candidate they felt could not win, nor to continue to inform their readers how the alternate candidates differed on the issues from the major candidates. The editors decided that Anderson, because he had a chance to win the horse race, in their opinions, and because he had a chance to raise millions of dollars, was also presenting the public an alternative on the issues to Carter and Reagan. I want to know if, in reality, people like David Garth specifically packaged Anderson to make Anderson appear as though he differed on the issues? I feel that a careful examination of Anderson's position papers and his speeches will reveal he basically did not differ on the issues from Reagan or Carter. Only his *image* differed. I also propose that Anderson got more ink and less votes than any third party candidate since George Wallace. What are your feelings about this from a journalist's standpoint, a journalist who was working for the *L.A. Times* Washington bureau at that point?

A.    I agree with Bradlee that it was decided Commoner did not have a chance, that Anderson did have a chance, and that it did not make sense to assign a reporter to cover someone who didn't have a chance, no matter how he might have differed on the issues or what sort of an alternative he might have provided to Reagan and Carter. I haven't seen your analysis of Anderson's differing positions but, as I remember it, he did differ quite strikingly with Carter and Reagan on some of the major issues. I can't say on all of them; I can't even recall which ones. As I remember it, he was a legitimate alternative to both of them.

Q.    So there you would disagree? You would feel it wasn't just image? You feel you could specifically point out where he disagreed totally with Reagan on an issue and totally with Carter on the same issue?

A.     Well, I can't remember specifically. But I do remember during the campaign that my own impression was that Anderson differed substantially enough from both Reagan and Carter to be considered an alternative.

Q.     Tom Wicker told me his feeling is that in dealing with the issue situation, he feels it isn't a journalist's role to in any way try and force the candidates to speak about issues. He feels that right now in this country, journalists are following along with what the polls are showing and with what the people want, that people want to deal with personalities, candidate's wives, and a lot of other personal things. He told Barry Commoner before Commoner was even nominated that, if he was going to run an issues-oriented campaign, he wouldn't have a chance. I'd like you to comment on that.

A.     Well, I think Wicker was right. I think if somebody runs strictly an issues campaign with no sort of gimmicks or no personality building at all in his campaign, that he is going to bore people to death. Carter and Reagan both used to complain during the 1980 election that reporters would seize on relatively minor things at times and not be concerned about the issues. Carter was really hung up on that, that the news media did not stick with the issues much. But at the same time, you can't keep people reading about the issues day in and day out. They just don't do it. If you don't find something in what he said that contradicts what he said the previous week or something that he says that is an outrageous kind of allegation concerning his opponent or something, you don't keep the reader's or the viewer's attention. In other words, you're not communicating.

Q.     In Commoner's case, he was never asked to be on "Face the Nation," "Issues and Answers," or "Meet the Press." He never was granted a long, in-depth, one-on-one front page piece in the *New York Times*, the *Wall Street Journal* or the *Los Angeles Times*, like the other candidates. I talked to Haynes Johnson of the *Washington Post* and he said that the *Post* did do a feature story on him, but what I want to probe with you, Jack, is when we look ahead to 1984, is there any way to break this cycle? Is there any way for the media perhaps to be a little less influenced by what the polls are showing, or by whether one candidate's personality is a little more exciting than another, and give a little more exposure to this type of a candidate, or do you just feel there will always be a 'Dr. Ben Spock' running, and you don't see anything changing for 1984?

A.      No, I really don't. I see there will always be the candidate who will come out and say I'm running and people will say okay but you don't stand a chance and so therefore you will never really get the kind of attention that the major candidates get. Now I do think that the media has done much better on covering issues. They did better in '80 than in '76 in my opinion, and better in '76 than in '72, and one reason is that newspapers, news magazines, the television networks — everybody, goes through the same exercise you are talking about right now. What is it we do wrong? Did we not give the reader or the viewer adequate information about the major issues and where the candidates stand? And so, as a result, if you look back at what we've done, I think you'll find that we've all treated the issues in great depth many times during the campaign. But as to treating a particular candidate like Benjamin Spock or Barry Commoner with the same amount of attention and space in the paper and time on the air as a major candidate no matter what they might say, you're just not going to do that because it's considered wasted space and a waste of time. You've only got so many resources. That's the point. You've got to have priorities. And your priorities are the candidates who have a chance to win.

Q.      The *Los Angeles Times* assigns a journalist to cover practically every national football league game on Sundays. If we have 12 people run for president in 1984, will the *Los Angeles Times* assign 12 people, one to cover each candidate?

A.      I would say no, unless it was considered that all of them had some sort of a reasonable chance of winning. I'll give you a perfect example right now of a candidate who may be going to run or says that he wants to run in 1984, and that is Alan Cranston, a terrific senator from the state of California, the Senate Democratic whip, and a man who is highly regarded in California, and highly regarded in Washington. He is not at this time considered to have any chance of winning, although we had a long story on page one when he said that he was naming an exploratory committee and so forth. We've had a couple of other stories about how he has gone out in the east and northeast to kind of 'test the waters', but if Alan Cranston doesn't one day take off in his race for the presidency, and most people think he's not going to, he won't get very much attention, even from his home town newspaper, the *Los Angeles Times*. They are not going to waste their space, time, effort and resources on a candidate whom they believe doesn't stand a chance even though they highly respect him as a senator.

Q.     *Life Magazine*, in their year end issue in 1980, had quotes from all of the candidates. A Los Angeles television newscaster asked Barry Commoner in a one-on-one 30-minute interview, 'Are you a serious candidate or are you just running on the issues?' Just an outrageous question like that. Wicker's response to me was that he didn't think that it was all that outrageous because he felt Commoner didn't have the money, and didn't have the same kind of personality that someone like Reagan had, who is very charismatic on television. No matter how brilliant or well-thought-out that platform may have been in Cleveland at the Citizens Party National Convention, there was no way Commoner was going to get the national news media to give him the same kind of attention they would give to a candidate they perceived as more likely to win.

A.     I agree with Wicker. I think that's right. No matter how right he may be on the issues, no matter how well he may articulate them, no matter how many people he may have who think that he has great credibility — either he does have, or is perceived as having, a reasonable chance to either win or to affect the race or he is not going to get the attention. That's just the way the game is played.

Q.     James Perry of the *Wall Street Journal* told me that what amazed him was that Clark sent all kinds of carefully-worded press releases, but that the Commoner office in Washington seldom sent him a press release and that this definitely influenced him as to whether he would do some kind of an interview with Clark or Commoner. I don't think he interviewed either of them, but this was his feeling. In other words, do you feel that the public relations aspect of candidates in a campaign is really important or should we say, "Hey! I don't care what kind of handouts Clark or Commoner is going to send me at the *Los Angeles Times*, we should go out and interview them and see what they have to say, and let the people decide from that point on?"

A.  Well, again, I think it's what sort of releases are going out, what sort of ads are being taken out, how much visibility a particular candidate is getting. The reason Clark got more attention than Commoner in the end, was not just because he got on 50 ballots, but it was because one way or the other he developed more resources and he did have a more professional operation. He was perceived as having a professional operation when the polls came out and showed him with four percent, or whatever it was, but with a lot more than Commoner. Even though he wasn't regarded as a serious threat, he was regarded as a more serious candidate than Commoner. I guess that's always the way it's going to be.

Q.  As you know, the *Voice* paid a lot of attention to Commoner and they endorsed him on the front page of the paper.

A.  They carry an enormous wallop!

Q.  Let me ask you this: In looking back at that campaign, in the meetings you had, and in the work you did for "Washington Week in Review," do you ever recall anyone, such as, Haynes Johnson or Jim Lehrer, or Paul Duke, discussing Barry Commoner or the Citizens party? Do you remember? It's going to test your memory; it's been quite awhile ago and the thing went on for a year and a half. Do you recall anyone saying, "Gee, we ought to do an interview with Commoner?"

A.  I don't remember Commoner ever being discussed, period!

Q.  Elizabeth Drew just published a long book about the campaign and never once in the book does she mention Barry Commoner's name. Additionally the *Washington Post* editors as you may recall, rushed out a quickie book after the election was over and never once was Barry Commoner's name mentioned. I'm just wondering about the inner workings of the *Los Angeles Times*. Someone told me that Bob Scheer was going to interview Commoner when he was speaking at the Wilshire Ebell Theater in Los Angeles and that, literally, the journalist didn't show up. Someone then said to Scheer, "Hey, we're not even sure Commoner is going to be on the ballot. We're going to hold off until after the conventions are over. We don't want you to do an interview right now." That's just some feedback I got.

A.     I wouldn't know whether it's true or not because it happened in L.A. and I'm in Washington. So I wouldn't know.

Q.     You don't recall any lobbying going on in your bureau? Someone saying to Lee May, "Hey, it's about time. We never did anything on Commoner, go out and write a story."

A.     I don't even know how he happened to have been given that assignment. I gather that someone from L.A. said that we need an interview with Commoner, and our news editor, Dick Cooper, said "Well, Lee May will do it."

Q.     So, from your insider's point of view on 'Washington Week' and at the *Times* Washington bureau, right from the beginning they just didn't feel Commoner had a chance, that Anderson was the third party candidate and that was it.

A.     That's right!

# PART III

# *The Media Remains Silent and Unreceptive*

Summary: Examines how the media remains unreceptive to giving coverage to the new 1984 Citizens party candidate, Sonia Johnson, a newsworthy candidate who focuses on major issues. Detailed accounts highlight the media's role in the political process and question their influence in determining the winners and losers in the political arena by their choice to cover only the two major political parties.

# "Citizens Party"
## *from the* Progressive,
## *October, 1982, p. 36-38*

### *by*
### *Marty Jezer*

After its disastrous 1980 presidential campaign, the Citizens party seemed to fade from the progressive political spectrum. Its presidential ticket of Barry Commoner and LaDonna Harris had run with the expectation of winning five percent of the popular vote, but finished with less than one percent — a dismal showing. More telling, the campaign failed to galvanize the constituencies it had tried to reach. The left was indifferent; labor, minorities, and the poor barely knew the party existed.

The party's one achievement was to involve a core group of experienced activists in chapters around the country. These were veterans of the radical movements of the 1960s and 1970s; no longer part of a transient subculture isolated from mainstream America, they were settled now, with neighborly ties to workplace and community. What drew these activists into the Citizens party was not the Commoner ticket, but the conclusion that alternative or counter-cultural politics, single-issue organizing, and direct-action campaigns (demonstrations, marches, civil disobedience) were *in themselves* no longer enough to build a radical movement.

Despite the 1980 debacle, these people remained committed to the idea of a third party. They have quietly gone on to build a number of strong local and statewide chapters. A few surprising victories have been won (in Burlington, Vermont; Seattle, Washington and Schenectady, New York), but even in defeat the party has made respectable showings. In Atlanta, for instance, John Sweet, with the support of John Lewis and Julian Bond, won 49.4 percent of the vote for an at-large city council seat. Elsewhere, the party has attracted 10 to 40 percent of the vote in locales where left wing parties never before counted for anything. This is encouraging, for it means that a radical third party committed to serious door-to-door campaigning *can* appeal to a non-radical electorate.

But the party is still attracting little attention — much less support — from the left. One obvious reason is the party's own enigmatic evolution. Another is American history. The left in the United States has long been indifferent to electoral politics, and any party that intends to enter the electoral flow has to wade up stream.

Henry Wallace's 1948 Progressive party presidential campaign was the old left's last hurrah. The pacifist ban-the-bombers who, during the late 1950s, revived the radical movements were ideologically opposed to electoral politics. Their philosophy of direct action, non-violent or otherwise, and alternative politics — building a new world in the shell of the old, as the wobblies once put it — has been a persistent if not dominate influence in the American left.

This attitude toward political action has been reinforced by the left's own electoral experience over the past 20 years. Voter registration coexisted with direct action during the early days of the civil rights movement, but the radicals of the new left saw the Democratic party's refusal to seat the Mississippi Freedom Democratic party at the 1964 Atlantic City national convention as an unforgivable betrayal. The police rampage at the 1968 national convention in Chicago and Hubert Humphrey's refusal to break with Lyndon Johnson's Vietnam policy merely confirmed the new left's estrangement from the democrats. There was a brief reconciliation in 1972 with the McGovern campaign but party regulars vowed that the new left forces would never wield power again.

Independent third parties, meanwhile, proved utterly inconsequential during this period. The quixotic presidential candidacies of Dr. Benjamin Spock and Dick Gregory left no on-going organizations. And, until the Citizens party, the left showed no sustained interest in local elections.

That leaves Michael Harrington and his democratic socialists who, virtually alone on the left, have been committed to the electoral framework. But their support of the Democratic party and their tactical approach to work within the party have isolated them from the activist-oriented left. Lobbying for a more progressive agenda at the top, Harrington's people have stayed clear of local politicking and grass-roots, socialist spadework. But the analysis that inspired the Citizens party — that the time for electoral action is now — works for Harrington as well. To the degree that the broad left finds electoral politics useful (and I would insist that it is the only direction the movement can possibly go), the Citizens party and Harrington's Democratic Socialists of America (DSA) are likely to become the most visible and effective players.

Unlike the Citizens party, the DSA, with its standing in the Democratic party, has an established niche. The people it is trying to educate do not first have to be persuaded to vote. By contrast, the Citizens party is an electoral upstart, breaking new ground as it attempts to move beyond its limited constituency. Superficially, the party would seem to have little going for it. Without any charismatic figure of national stature (except for Commoner), with no history or tradition to rally its forces (even in the dullest of times, socialists can recall a heyday with Debs and Thomas, and rouse themselves with 'The Internationale'), with an ambiguous ideology (the party's call for economic democracy, after all, is an obfuscation of socialist ideas), and, as a result, a perplexing self-image, it's no wonder the party has been hard put to generate much excitement.

These limitations would be inherent in any new movement, but special difficulties for the Citizens party are grounded in the popular misconception that it is the Barry Commoner party, an environmentalist clique composed mainly of granola-munching ecology activists. To be sure, this was a preconception that many *in* the party held. Rejecting the image for themselves, they worried that it was the makeup of the party everywhere else. It was only at the national convention in New York this past May (the first nationwide gathering of party stalwarts since the 1980 founding convention) that members were able to take a true measure of themselves.

The three hundred or so delegates from 30 states were distinguishable by their rootedness and age. There were few students; little effort had been made to recruit them. Most delegates were 30 and over. Teachers, social and human service workers, small entrepreneurs, and similar new class occupations predominated. But there was also a smattering of blue-collar workers, indicative of a newly proletarianized, downwardly mobile middle-class. Politically, members have been democrats, Marxist-Leninists and everything in between. But the grass roots perspective encourages pragmatism. The fine line between economic democracy and democratic socialism is not a raging issue. What's important is how to become credible to the mass of American people.

As for Commoner, pigeonholing him as an environmentalist has always been unfair. He has consistently brought his ecological insights to other concerns; indeed, he was one of the first environmental scientists to work with labor on workplace safety. Moreover, as spokesman for the party, he has steadily emphasized economic, peace, and foreign policy issues. Yet, he has also tried to distance himself and the party from the more traditional left.

It was at Commoner's initiative that the party sought to identify itself with the "green" or ecology parties of the European dimension, akin to DSA's participation in the Socialist International, but the European Greens come out of a sophisticated, electorally oriented, mass-based left. In the United States, where this context doesn't exist, the green idea tends to translate into elementary environmentalism, which only reinforces the initial misconception of the party's narrow focus. The radical ecology activists, who identify with the Greens, are generally the most adamant in belittling the vote. On the local level, where the party members can articulate their positions face-to-face, confusion over what the party stands for is not a problem. But in the national arena, where media politics holds sway, the ambiguity thrives.

Still, it was apparent at the national convention that the party had matured. In two years it has transformed itself from the Barry Commoner party to an organizer's party. The local chapters are in control. Politics flows from the bottom up and the party will go wherever its members choose to take it. The chapters have developed independently of one another, yet a consensus exists to emphasize local and statewide elections.

But, can an organizer's party be an authentic citizens party in the absence of a radicalized base? Organizing among feminists, trade-unionists and politically conscious Hispanics and blacks is not the same as building mass support. In originally planning to organize among the near majority who do not vote, the party had hoped to create a base of its own, but this was a romantic notion. People who don't vote don't go to demonstrations, either. Mostly, they are resigned and apathetic, alienated from politics of every kind. Only a patient and sustained effort can politicize them. It would seem, then, that an electoral party of the kind we have in the United States (as opposed to the European parties with their social and cultural components) is not the best consciousness-raising tool except, perhaps, where the Citizens party has so far been most effective — on the local level.

Seen from this angle, much of what appears to be weakness in the Citizens party turns out to be a seedbed of strength. The absence of compelling personalities creates openings for new leadership. The weakness of the national leadership and the relative cohesion of local chapters make participatory decision-making not only possible but necessary. Even the party's dreary image has a brighter side. Its triumphs, such as they are, are substantive. Rock stars and media personalities have not taken to the hustings on the party's behalf. Instead, party members have been slugging it out in the boondocks, meeting America on its own terms. The Citizens party cannot be accused of radical chic.

The absence of labor support remains a pressing problem. Many leftists who believe in third party politics are aloof from the Citizens party because it lacks a base in the traditional working class. But fact is fact. The Democratic party (as the DSA might argue) is *the* labor party and there is no evidence that the AFL-CIO is ready to make a historic break from the Kennedys and Mondales of this world. The Citizens party certainly should do more work with the rank-and-file and dissident movements. But even progressive trade unionists are not likely to join the party until it wins more elections and proves that it has the clout to do something for them. In the meantime, the party does not block the way for a labor-base party. That this is not the time for such a party does not automatically make party building premature.

Much the same can be said with regard to the organizing of blacks, Hispanics, and other minority groups. The Citizens party is overwhelmingly white. The party constitution mandates affirmative action, but it is unlikely that party leadership, in the foreseeable future, can be racially balanced. The party has the choice of guilt-tripping itself for its pallid complexion, as is customary on the left, or continuing to organize where it's most capable.

At the national convention, Yolanda Sanchez and Herbert Daughtry were virtually the only representatives of minority groups in sight. Sanchez has been active in the New York chapter but now devotes herself to organizing in the Puerto Rican community. Daughtry is head of the city's Black United Front. From the podium, both made essentially the same points: that the Citizens party should not expect to organize successfully in minority areas; that minority groups first have to organize themselves. In the interim, multiracial coalitions are possible, and the Citizens party should continue its work. "When we are ready to move, we want you to be there," Daughtry said. Progressive trade unionists might say the same.

More serious than racial imbalance is the party's male predominance. Bringing women into the party is the most immediate, important challenge. At the New York convention, the delegates voted to fund a national organizer's position to recruit women. The party already had strict rules requiring a balance of women and men in leadership ranks. But where the rules have been followed, women have had to be recruited; men, as usual, readily step forward.

The future of the party lies in continuing to build a decentralized infrastructure while focusing on local and state races where respectable showings are possible without heavy media expenditures. Do party members have the discipline to stick to that formula? Here again, party attitudes reflect common shortcomings of the left. Local issues pale before grave matters of war and peace. Local issues are detail ridden and rarely invite emotionally satisfying radical solutions.

Consequently, candidates tend to prefer hopeless national races (where they can raise the big issues) and shun local races where personal canvassing counts and the issues are relatively mundane. This November, (1982) the party is planning to contest (at mid-summer count) more than 80 local and state races in at least 20 states. Another 20 or so candidates are planning to run for the U.S. Senate and House.

Conservative and moderate democrats are the most likely targets. In Vermont, the Burlington victory came against an entrenched and conservative democratic machine. Going after liberal democrats is problematic, especially on the federal level. The need to make the party visible and raise progressive issues, must be weighed against the possibility of spoiling the victory of a liberal whose vote on specific issues (El Salvador, abortion) might be critical.

Whether or not to challenge a liberal democrat is best decided on the local level. But the party is emotionally committed to taking on *all* democrats. This was made clear at the national convention when the question of cross-endorsements was up for debate. Speaker after speaker denounced working with liberal democrats, though characteristically, when a vote on the matter was taken, pragmatism won out and the party resolved to discourage rather than prohibit cross-endorsements. "What!" exclaimed one Bay Area delegate, "We can't support Ron Dellums?"

The prospects of the party may still turn on its ability to break the movement of its exclusive interest in direct action and woo activists to electoral politics instead. Time and again the left has mobilized hundreds of thousands of people for one cause or another. But it has never been able to translate crowds into permanent organizations that can compete for power. A case in point, perhaps is the June 12 disarmament rally in New York, when more than eight hundred thousand people marched for the nuclear freeze.

Where does that movement go from there? It can be the question and call for a second larger demonstration. It can also up the ante with militant tactics, but risk losing moderate supporters. The only other course is electoral activity to influence the Democratic party or build an independent third party.

Participation in electoral politics *must* become part of movement strategy; direct action by itself is a dead end. Whether it's more fruitful to work in the Citizens party or to organize, as Harrington insists, within the Democratic party, can only be determined over time. At this point, it is important only that the Citizens party and the DSA do not compete.

As long as the Citizens party emphasizes party building at the grass roots (and the DSA refrains from running candidates), a rivalry need not become troublesome, or even arise. But on the national level, where the Citizens party is bound sooner or later to go after DSA-backed candidates, the two organizations will have to agree to disagree in this limited field while making conscientious efforts to cooperate in every other respect.

The Citizens party has to be taken seriously. It is finally doing what it set out to do — become a decentralized, democratic, progressive party. It has won some victories and has set up chapters that show every sign of growing. Only time will tell whether the party will ultimately become the electoral arm of the American left. It is groundwork time now.

# Green Party Inspires
# U.S. Environmentalists

## Whole Life Times, *June 1983*

The recent election of the Green party — coalition of environmentalists, anti-nuclear power and disarmament activists, feminist, and other like-minded political groups — to five percent of the seats in the West German parliament has excited and challenged similar groups on this side of the Atlantic. Could it work here?

"A 'Green Revolution' has already begun," Chris Cook, administrative director Greenpeace, says optimistically. "It's just a matter of time before it gains widespread recognition and policymakers realize people want that. Environmental groups are already lobbying and campaigning for candidates sympathetic to the idea of ecology. Once we have a Times Beach (dioxin disaster) in every state, I think we'll see a revolt around the political structure."

One big advantage that has helped the Greens to emerge in West Germany's proportional representation system is that losing parties get representatives based on their percentage of the vote. In contrast, U.S. environmental groups, such as the Sierra Club and Friends of the Earth, have opted to put their energy into political action committees (PAC), supporting major candidates instead of trying to run their own. But at least one group — Commoner's Citizens party — hopes to emulate the Greens. "We don't accept a lot of money from PACs, so we can stay strong and keep to our platform," says Wendy Adler, the party's national director.

Now four years old — the same age as the Green party — the Citizens party has elected 10 local candidates, four of which are in Burlington, Vermont. The party hopes to run some strong congressional races in 1983 and is beginning to consider candidates.

# The Significant Alternatives
## *the* Progressive, *1983*

### *by*
### *Sidney Lens*

In 1984, as so often in the past, many millions of American people will have to express themselves at the ballot box.

Those who want an end to the arms race, a reduction of arms, and a transfer of military money to human needs, will find that the difference between both traditional political parties, and between all the candidates, is merely on how much *to increase* military spending. None, not even those who call for a nuclear freeze, have suggested that we can live with half or a quarter of the incredible sums now spent on armaments that are bleeding our country white.

None has expressed the moral courage that many Catholic bishops have in stating, that the mere production of weapons of mass murder is a sin or a crime against humanity. None speaks in terms of the ultimate abolition of nuclear weapons, or indeed of the conventional weapons that are more and more developing a capability to kill, that approximates the capability of small atomic devices.

On this, the most important issue facing Americans and the human race, there is no one in the Democratic or Republican parties who hears our pleas or expresses our despair. If we waste another four years by voting for candidates or a political party that is not as bad as the other, we only head towards Armageddon with greater celerity.

The only way a progressive or radical citizen can express his fears and concerns on the arms race is to vote for the Citizens party; a small party, it is true, but one which stands for disarmament not rearmament; for abolition of nuclear weapons, not arms control.

Millions of Americans face a similar dilemma about their economic well being. There is no way to express our demand for full employment, for curbing the power of the corporations and multinationals, for a redistribution of national income in favor of those who need it most rather than those who need it least, than to vote for the Citizens party.

Despite brief periodic upturns from recent recessions, it is clear that militarism and corporate greed have undermined our economy to the point where we seem to be headed, at one and the same time both, to holocaust and economic bankruptcy. There is no way a citizen can object at the ballot box in 1984 because all the candidates and both political parties are committed to retaining the present corporate structure.

Although some candidates are more liberal than others, all — without exception — accept the sanctity of the present economic order. None favors economic planning, social ownership of certain basic industries, and social control of others. Such sensible planks, without which our economy cannot right itself, are derogated as socialist and are dismissed. In fact, they are only common sense, just as economic planning and social sharing is common sense for a family.

We are now living in a revolutionary age. Scores of countries are in the midst of a national revolution; new technology is changing our lives more dramatically than ever before. The military revolution threatens us with annihilation as never before.

In these circumstances, we must make sharp departures from the past.

The Citizens party offers such a departure. It is a party that works to elect people committed to a drastically new program, but even more, a party that believes in accountability. Under present circumstances, it makes no difference who you vote for or what program he or she has pledged to carry out beforehand. Almost no one — and certainly not our presidents — lives up to such promises or is even expected to.

We therefore, have not a two party system but a 537 party system. Each congressperson, senator or president and vice-president is a party unto themselves. Since there is no accountability, we do not know for whom or what we are voting.

The Citizens party, believes that it must work with and be part of that great movement of the injured and oppressed who take their complaints to the street; the unemployed and homeless, the tens of millions who fear war; the blacks, Spanish-speaking and native Americans; the women who are half our population but are still second-class citizens; and the organized workers — 22 million strong — who have been forced by the last two administrations to give back benefits they have worked so hard to win.

"We, the Citizens party, will fight for these under-privileged at the ballot box and in the legislatures. We will march side-by-side with them in their strikes, picket lines, vigils and lobby caravans — for they are the constituency we want to represent and be identified with — no other."

This is the approach of the Citizens party to American politics for 1984. For those who believe fervidly in peace and justice, we believe this party represents their hopes and aspirations.

We also believe we offer the only real alternative, the only way a dedicated citizen can vote without wasting his vote, without wasting another four years.

The Citizens party has a comprehensive program: civil rights, the environment, solar energy, civil liberties and conservation as well as on peace and disarmament. We invite those who seek an end to the arms race and corporate domination of our lives to join us in the 1984 electoral campaign because the Citizens party is the only significant alternative to the politics of yesterday and to the politics of holocaust and economic bankruptcy.

# The Politics of 1984

## by
### Barry Commoner

*Address before the Convention of
the Citizens party
San Francisco, California, September 3, 1983*

We meet here, in convention, just four years after the decision to create the Citizens party. In these four years a great deal has happened in the political life of the country. In that time the Citizens party has become an authentic part of American politics, small but meaningful, vigorous and growing.

It is helpful to remember that the 1980 presidential campaign gave us not only Ronald Reagan, but perhaps to atone for that mistake, the campaign also gave birth to the Citizens party. We are here today to talk about what we ought to do in the 1984 campaign, which I hope and believe will mark the end of Reagan's political career without, if we are smart about it, doing the same for the Citizens party.

We in the Citizens party have two responsibilities. One is to participate in the election in a way that helps to explain the problems that confront the country, and how they can be solved in the interest of the American people. The second responsibility is to build the strength of the Citizens party by increasing our public support and using our still-limited resources wisely.

These two responsibilities are closely linked. The party can win more public support only if we help the American people fight, and if possible win, their political battles.

In 1980 the country faced political issues which the Democratic and Republican parties were equally unable to discuss sensibly, let alone solve: the rapid deterioration of the economy, continued discrimination against women and minorities, inadequate social, environmental and energy programs and the growing threat of a suicidal nuclear war. Our response was to campaign on a program of economic as well as political democracy, based on our belief that to solve these problems the American people must govern the system of production and the economy, democratically, in the interest of the national welfare rather than corporate profit. And we asserted that both the national economy and world peace required the drastic reduction of the military budget.

In 1980, in response to this political analysis, we concluded, quite properly in my opinion, that the best way to develop public discussion of these basic political issues and to build the Citizens party was to run a national presidential campaign in as many states as possible. Events since 1980 have confirmed the importance of that decision and have demonstrated the value of the presidential campaign in building the party. The very fact that we got on the ballot in 30 states and conducted a national campaign only one year after our founding, put the party and its program in place in the U.S. political scene. The state-by-state campaign for ballot access created the state organizations which have since then conducted nearly two hundred local campaigns and have elected 11 Citizens party candidates to office.

Now, in deciding what to do in the 1984 campaign, we must again start with an evaluation of the country's political problems before we consider how the Citizens party can best participate in the effort to solve them. There are at present three basic facts about American politics.

First, it is a fact — a tragic, appalling fact — that Ronald Reagan has willfully caused grievous harm to the American people: to working people, to blacks, Asians and Hispanics, to women, to the kids trying to get some nourishment out of their school lunches, to their grandparents trying to remain healthy on Medicare, and to all of us who breathe the polluted air and drink the tainted water. Ronald Reagan has willfully harmed our neighbors in Nicaragua, harassed the people of El Salvador and Granada, and has spread malice and fear around the globe. Reagan's malevolent policies are so ingrained in his party's positions that they will be the major political issue in 1984, whether he or someone else heads the Republican ticket. The dominant political issue in 1984 is to defeat Ronald Reagan; to repudiate his evil policies, for the sake of the welfare of the American people and the peace of the world.

Second, it is a fact — a fact that would be funny if it were not so grimly serious — that the Democratic party's candidates, the Sad Six, are unable, and more than likely unwilling, to offer the country any meaningful alternative to Reagan's policies. Their main political virtue is simple: They are not Ronald Reagan. But this is hardly an adequate basis for defeating Reagan's *policies*.

The leaders of the Democratic party have prepared for the 1984 campaign by systematically *destroying* their ability to oppose Reagan's policies. It will be very difficult for the democratic candidates to convince voters that they can reverse the cuts in welfare programs when voters remember that it was the democratic majority in the House that passed Reagan's 1980 budget and transferred some $40 billion from social services to the military. It will be very difficult for the democratic candidates to persuade us that unlike Reagan, they respect the right of Latin American countries to choose their own governments, when they have failed, in Congress, to expose the Reagan administration's illegal assault on the government of Nicaragua.

Not one of the Democratic party's announced candidates is untainted by support for at least some of Reagan's disastrous policies: On the freeze, Glenn is nearly indistinguishable from Reagan; Cranston is all for the freeze but he supports the B-1 bomber; Hart and Mondale want to limit nuclear weapons — and increase conventional ones. Nowhere among the democratic candidates is there the slightest sign of an eagerness, or even a willingness, to really take

Reagan on and denounce his administration for what it is: an outrageous, immoral, often illegal assault on the poor and the weak; on the environment; on world peace. It is a fact that we cannot rely on the Democratic party's announced candidates to do what most Americans want done in 1984 — to repudiate Reagan's disastrous policies and retire him from office.

The third political fact is the surprising strength of the people's progressive movements: for civil rights, peace, sexual equality, the environment, energy, and the sensible use of resources. Repeatedly the Reagan administration has been confronted by this strength: labor's great solidarity march in 1982; the huge peace march in New York last June 12; the great gathering in memory of Martin Luther King, Jr., in Washington last week; the massive defection of women from Reagan's policies; the continuing support, despite Reagan's efforts to undercut them, for environmental, anti-nuclear and solar programs. All this makes it clear that there is deep-seated opposition to Reagan's policies. And it is significant that all of these movements arose spontaneously, among the people; not one of them has been inspired by a conventional political leader. Neither Martin Luther King, Jr., nor Rachel Carson, nor any feminist leader, was a member of the political establishment.

Another striking feature of these popular movements is that they are concerned with fundamental, *moral* issues. The civil rights movement and the women's movement assert that it is wrong for people to be treated unequally because of their color or their sex. The environmental movement asserts that it is wrong to destroy the environment which must support us and future generations. The energy movement asserts that it is wrong to run our economy, which crucially depends on energy, on irreplaceable, non-renewable sources. The peace movement asserts that it is wrong, in the name of defense, to threaten the human race with suicide.

Compare the force of these people's issues with the issues on which conventional politicians run for office. Should we increase the military budget a lot or only a little? Should we give the corporations a big tax break, or only a little one? Should we send a battle force to Latin America, or just advisers?

The conventional politicians skate on the surface of the questions that really trouble people. The popular movements deal with basic questions that cut to the heart of what this country is all about. At the bottom, every one of these movements is concerned with the same fundamental question: who is running the country, and in whose interest? These, I believe, are the political facts. Before we consider what the Citizens party should do, it is useful to review some facts about ourselves. The first fundamental fact is that we exist; that the 1980 campaign created the Citizens party and that since then its members, in more than 20 states, are engaged in politics, with increasingly successful results. And it is also a fact that our political successes since 1980 have been based almost entirely on local activity; as a national organization, the Citizens party has been nearly invisible. The national office has managed to raise enough money to just about keep going; and for this we owe a debt of gratitude to Rick LaRue and Wendy Adler. It has put out a few issues of the *Citizens Voice*, but has been able to do little else. In particular, as a national entity the Citizens party has thus far failed to take its rightful place in the broad spectrum of popular movements.

These facts tell us that on both fronts — the U.S. political scene and the state of the Citizens party — there have been important changes between 1980 and now. In 1980 the overriding political issue was the failure of both parties and all the conventional candidates (including John Anderson) to confront the need for fundamental new approach to the governance of the system of production, which, as it crumbles, is destroying the livelihood of whole cities (Youngstown, Ohio; Buffalo, New York; and Wheeling, West Virginia) and devastating entire industries: steel, auto and railroads.

We should keep in mind that in 1980 our campaign for breaking the corporate grip on America, for economic democracy, was not an abstract exercise in political ideology; a source of personal pride in our true-blue (or should I say red) radicalism. Yes, a fundamental change in the economic system — economic democracy — is a basic precept of Citizens party ideology. But we must never forget that the purpose of that ideology is to improve the lives of real people, in particular the poor and disenfranchised.

Today the fundamental problem of economic democracy remains unsolved, but what that problem means to the American people is that we must stop Reagan's cruel campaign against the very people who suffer the most from their lack of economic power, from the absence of economic democracy.

The political life of the Citizens party has also changed. In 1980, the strength of the Citizens party derived from the presidential campaign, which created the state organizations and readied them for local campaigns. Since 1980, the Citizens party has grown almost entirely through the local political campaigns that have given us victories from Texas to Vermont.

What, then, should we do now? How can we participate in the central political issue of the day — defeating Reagan — and yet point out the inadequacy of the Democratic party and carry forward the essential campaign for economic democracy? This is the primary question, for unless we do serve the essential political interests of the American people we will not merit their support and we cannot build the Citizens party.

There is today a great political vacuum in the country. The series of movement activities, climaxed by the great march in Washington last week, tell us that major segments of the American people — a potential majority — are fed up, not only with Reagan's callous cynicism but with the bumbling, pussyfooting democratic candidates. This leaves a vacuum, but a vacuum charged with a deep unmet desire for a political program that will smash Reagan's phony facade and expose the democrats' impotence.

If nothing new happens between now and the multi-million dollar charade of primaries next spring, the political vacuum will be filled by the issues that the television networks think look good on the tube (and sell): Does Reagan dye his hair or not? Was Glenn airsick when he circled the globe? Is Mondale's brother (if he has one) drinking beer with some foreign types? Once again the election of the president will be determined by public relations instead of politics. Once again the fate of the country will be in the hands of hucksters — the Garth's, the Cadell's, and the Nofziger's. Once again discussion of the issues will be carefully staged by the League of Women Voters, with high marks going to the candidate that does the best job of ducking them. Once again, the progressive movements will have no way to express the nation's hunger for economic and social justice, for peace, for simple human decency. Once again, half the American voters will have good reason to stay home on election day. Once again, we will witness the death of politics in America.

But there is at this moment one sign of hope; that a black leader in the bitter battle for civil rights, a courageous fighter for the poor and the oppressed, Jesse Jackson, may be willing to take on both the democrats' Sad Six *and* Ronald Reagan. Jesse Jackson knows that the interests of blacks, of the poor, are fundamentally related to the interests of women, of environmentalists, of everyone who hopes to survive the nuclear age. He wants to build a Rainbow Coalition, to merge these interests and to unite the movements into a crusade that will undertake as its first mission sending Ronald Reagan back to the ranch, this time for good.

I am convinced that at this moment in our political history, the needs and the hopes of progressive Americans can best be served by urging Jesse Jackson to run; to run against the democrats' Sad Six *and* Ronald Reagan, and when he does run, to help him do it.

If Jesse Jackson decides to run in the democratic primary, it will not be in response to some inner struggle for powerful force that lies far outside the reach of the Democratic party — the pent-up desire of the American people for honest politics — for politics that openly confronts the real issues of economic and social justice — that reawakens the country's conscience — that touches the heart of the body politic.

These are the interests of the Citizens party and the progressive movements, the basis of the Rainbow Coalition that Jesse Jackson calls for.

That is why I am convinced that the best thing we in the Citizens party can do, right now, to advance the cause of economic democracy, of social justice, of peace — the issues which gave birth to the Citizens party, and have sustained its life — is to join with all of progressive America and do everything we can to support Jesse Jackson's campaign to become the Democratic party's nominee for president in 1984.

What business, you will say, does the Citizens party have to support a democrat? Would we not betray our belief that neither party can serve the interests of the American people?

Well, *if* a huge progressive Rainbow Coalition builds around Jesse Jackson's candidacy, and *if* running on the coalition's progressive platform he wins the election and becomes the first black president of the United States — then I think we would need to re-examine that conviction. I, for one, have a strong enough belief in the need for an independent party, for the Citizens party, that I am quite willing to test it against the likelihood that all these things will happen.

Apart from the outcome of Jesse Jackson's candidacy, I think that the country needs a Rainbow Coalition. If it is created, it will be a large step toward the kind of politics that we in the Citizens party believe in and want to participate in. If it should then succeed in capturing the Democratic party, that will be progress. If not, it will still be an enormously progressive step, because it will have created a vastly more powerful base for an independent, third party.

But the immediate reason for supporting Jesse Jackson is that his campaign to register black and minority voters is the best hope that we have to defeat Ronald Reagan in 1984. In 1980, in many places in the country — enough to have turned the election around — the number of *un*registered black voters greatly exceeded Reagan's margin of victory over Carter. If, as I am convinced we must, we in the Citizens party must undertake to help the people of the United States defeat Reagan, we can do that best, at this time, by participating in Jesse Jackson's registration drive and in the political campaign that will give that drive its motivating force.

There was a time when such a move on the part of the Citizens party could be misunderstood. Four years ago it was sometimes hard to convince people that we were, indeed, an independent party and not some sort of temporary disaffection from the Democratic party. Now, nearly two hundred local campaigns and 11 victories later, we don't need to convince anyone that the Citizens party is, in fact, independent. The greater need now is to convince people that we are *relevant* — a meaningful factor in American politics.

For all these reasons I believe that the Citizens party, along with every other progressive group that belongs in a Rainbow Coalition, should work hard to support Jesse Jackson's campaign to register new voters and to develop what I hope will become his campaign for the democratic nomination.

What then? If Jesse Jackson runs for president as the democratic nominee, with the support of the Rainbow Coalition, will it make sense for the Citizens party to campaign against him? That question answers itself: of course not! If not Jesse Jackson, but one of the Sad Six runs, we will face a much more difficult question, which we must consider here, today. Here are some of the problems we have to think about.

First, we need to think about the political meaning of running our own candidate when the main issue that confronts the American people and which will surely dominate the concerns of progressive Americans — our constituency — is the repudiation of Reagan and his inhumane policies. At the very least, the Citizens party will be seen as failing to understand the country's political problems. At the worst, we will be seen as perhaps understanding these problems but for our own peculiar reasons unwilling, at this moment, to help solve them.

In turn, this political problem leads to a very practical one. If the Citizens party launches a national presidential campaign in 1984, we will need to do at least the same amount of work as we did in 1980 simply to get on the ballot and to conduct a national election campaign. And *in addition*, we will need to conduct, simultaneously, several hundred local campaigns to continue developing what is at present our only source of strength. These tasks will be much greater than what we had to do in 1980. Yet, realistically, we must expect less support from our friends and potential constituents for a presidential campaign than we had in 1980. The overall outcome is likely to be a smaller vote in the presidential election for the Citizens party than we received in 1980, and a falling off in the effort for local campaigns.

It seems to me that no matter what we decide to do, we face a dilemma which is a political fact of life. It means that if we *do not* run a presidential campaign, we lose the opportunity it would provide to help the American people understand the real issues that face the country. It means that if we *do* run a presidential campaign, we lose the support of our own constituents and hurt our local campaigns.

If we decide what to do in 1984 simply by choosing between running or not running a national presidential campaign, there is no way of avoiding either one of these costs. We would then need to decide which of these two alternatives would be the less damaging one. My own answer to that question is this: Because the welfare of the Citizens party depends on how well it helps the American people fight the crucial political battles, and because in 1984 that means helping to defeat Reaganism, we should not run a national political campaign and instead concentrate all our efforts on congressional, state and local races.

But I believe that there is a way to avoid this hard choice, a way to get the benefits of running a presidential campaign *without* losing the support of our constituents and *without* hurting our local campaigns. That is the purpose of what has been called the Vermont strategy.

The reasoning behind the proposal is this. The idea is to run a presidential campaign only in Vermont, but run to get a substantial proportion of the vote, and maybe to win. This is realistic in Vermont because we are already relatively strong there and because it is the one state in which we could use the electoral technique that has worked so well for us: meeting *all* the voters face to face. In a state with a high proportion of independent voters, such a campaign would enable us to demonstrate to the country what a real issue-oriented campaign would look like, while the rest of the country reacts in disgust to the huge cost of the conventional, empty, boring, media-oriented democratic and republican campaigns. Our Vermont campaign would dramatize what's wrong with conventional politics and how far it has departed from the goal of real, participatory democracy of the sort that the Citizens party believes in and practices.

This strategy would eliminate the difficult, costly state-by-state campaigns to get on as many state ballots as possible. Instead, state and local Citizens party organizations could concentrate their efforts on their own campaigns, including targeted campaigns for congress. These campaigns could be helped by visits from our presidential candidate, who could talk about the national issues and report on the progress in Vermont. Together, the congressional, state and local campaigns and the presidential campaign in Vermont would attract the support, for the Citizens party, of the people who like our program and are at the same time committed to defeating Reagan.

The Vermont strategy would also show that the Citizens party has the imagination and the courage to make a useful innovation in

American politics. Instead of taking on the two parties on *their* terms, where they are strongest — competing hopelessly for money and national media attention, for example — we enter the campaign on our own favorable terms and conduct it in a way that shows up the conventional campaigns for what they are: money-ridden perversions of real electoral democracy.

To those of our friends who would worry that a national presidential campaign by the Citizens party could help elect Reagan, we can point out that Vermont's three electoral votes are unlikely to make a difference. And, if it should turn out that the national vote is so close that Vermont's electoral votes do make the difference, we could (if we won them) pledge them to the democrats, in return for a position in the Cabinet — a move that might begin to push the United States in the direction of the more representative governments that make independent politics so much easier in European countries.

Such a strategy may be useful beyond the interests of the Citizens party. Jesse Jackson faces the same problem that we do: that running in the primary, and certainly, if he is defeated there, as an independent, would do serious damage to the chances of defeating Reagan. This argument is simply false with respect to the primary. On the contrary, if Jesse Jackson runs in the primary, millions of new voters, all committed to defeating Reagan, will be brought into the 1984 campaign. And given their lack of political appeal, if one of the conventional democratic candidates wins the nomination, these new voters are likely to be the crucial element in defeating Reagan. But, if an independent campaign should emerge from Jesse Jackson's run in the primary, it will face the same dilemma as the Citizens party and, as in our case, the answer may be a Mississippi or Alabama strategy.

The Citizens party and all of progressive America face a long and complex historic passage between now and November 1984. We cannot now predict what will happen on election day and beyond. But we do know that the outcome of the 1984 election — not only the name and party affiliation of the next president of the United States, but more importantly, the political strength of progressive America — depends crucially on how we start down that road, on what we do now.

I deeply believe that the place to start, now, is with Jesse Jackson's campaign. No matter how far it goes, Jesse Jackson's effort to breathe life into American politics, his courageous challenge to both the Republican and Democratic parties, is our best hope for a new beginning down the historic road to economic democracy, social justice, and peace.

# Let a Black Democrat Run for President
## Washington Post, 1983

### by
### Jesse L. Jackson

The fundamental relationship between blacks and the Democratic party must be renegotiated. No longer can blacks allow democrats to take them and their votes for granted. Power and responsibility must be shared fully, or the delicate balance of the traditional democratic coalition will be destroyed.

This is clear to most blacks but some democrats seems to have gotten the message. That is one reason why it would be a good idea to run a black candidate for the democratic presidential nomination in 1984. Such a move will force the democrats now (and the republicans later) to have a greater appreciation of the black vote and its potential positive contribution to party politics and the nation.

The idea of running a black for president is a hot topic among black leaders and is exciting the black masses across the country, because so many of them are unhappy with the current arrangements. Now it is all too common to hear white democrats telling blacks what is best for them, while reminding blacks that they have nowhere to go outside the Democratic party.

For democrats, race is increasingly becoming a litmus test of their party's true intentions. In the last year black democrats have won primaries in South Carolina, North Carolina, Mississippi, California, and Chicago; yet significant numbers of white democratic leaders and voters have chosen to support white republicans over those black democrats. If black people and their leaders support democrats without regard to race but others cannot reciprocate, then the character and viability of the party must be called into question.

With regard to a black presidential candidacy, there are four critical questions to be considered. Why run? What would such a candidacy require? What would be the advantages? What are the arguments against such a candidacy?

Why run? Blacks have their backs against the wall. The are increasingly distressed by the erosion of past gains and the rapidly deteriorating conditions within black and poor communities. As black leaders have attempted to remedy these problems through the Democratic party — of which black voters have been the most loyal and disciplined followers — too often they have been ignored or treated with disrespect. Mounting a serious presidential candidacy is one way of insisting that black leaders play significant roles and help shape policy and programs for the party.

Presently, many democrats are looking at 1984 and wondering how they can win back the swing voters who went for Jimmy Carter in 1976 but preferred Ronald Reagan in 1980. This ambition has led some democrats to the strategy formally outlined by Hamilton Jordan and Bert Lance. They have advised democrats to de-emphasize issues of primary concern to blacks, Hispanics, women and peace activists to give highest priority to recruiting the southern white conservative vote.

This amounts to pursuing the old republican strategy in the South, and it is the wrong way to go. To win a meaningful victory in 1984, the democrats must reach large numbers of the 75 million adult Americans who voted for no candidate in 1980, but went fishing instead. That huge group — 46 percent of the adult population — could be the key to building a new progressive coalition that would put the democrats back in the White House and in control of the senate.

Eighteen million eligible black voters can be the cornerstone of a new *coalition of the rejected* (the real silent majority) that can create new political options in 1984. The coalition would draw also on six million Hispanics, six million young people graduating from high school this year and next, women, more than half a million native Americans, 20 to 40 million poor whites, and those white liberals and moderates who would respond to an appeal to moral decency and enlightened economic self-interest.

But no such coalition can be built if democrats pursue the Jordan-Lance strategy. Instead of shying away from issues that would appeal to the most needy and deserving citizens — issues like a plan for full employment, affirming action that gives genuine opportunities to women, Hispanics and blacks, and strong enforcement of the Voting Rights Act to make democracy real for everyone — a successful democratic candidate should be emphasizing them. A black candidate could show the way.

A black candidate does not mean an exclusive black agenda, but an *inclusive* agenda that grows out of the black experience in America. Life viewed from a black perspective encompasses much more of America's interests and people than life viewed from the white, middle-class, male perspective; the perspective of our current leadership.

Rep. Shirley Chisholm (d.N.Y.) ran a serious campaign for president in 1976, but she did not enjoy the organized support of a broad coalition of groups. In 1984 we need an institutionally sponsored candidate who can argue not only the obvious economic issues, but also speak out against the corporate rape of blacks and Hispanics, against bloated military budgets, and against the cynical diplomacy that fosters alliances with corrupt and oppressive foreign governments like South Africa's. Such a candidate could speak out consistently for human rights; the same rights for Polish workers, the blacks of southern Africa, the peoples of the Middle East, the Caribbean and Latin America.

We must measure all human rights by one yardstick, and take into account the emerging world order. America contains only six percent of the world's population. Most of the world is black, brown, red and yellow, and poor. Much as we'd like everyone else to be like us, they're not; most people in the world don't speak English; most are not Christians. But they are all members of the human family. We must adjust from being superior over the world to being equivalent with it; and sometimes dependent on it.

A black candidate should have positions on all major issues, and not let other politicians and the media determine what issues are *appropriate* for black politicians to raise. As things stand, these issues will not be in the forefront of 1984 democratic debates, so we must devise our own vehicle to carry them to the country. We cannot ride to freedom in Pharoah's chariot.

A black should run to gain political victories, but that is not the only justification for this effort. A serious black candidate would help us gain collective self-respect and recognition. This is particularly important in terms of the young. Fully one-fourth of eligible black voters in 1984 will be 18 to 24. Those young people have no heroes among the other democratic candidates, and are unlikely to participate in 1984 unless they see an exciting new reason to do so. The best reason would be an effective black candidate.

Bargainers without bases are beggars, not brokers. Primaries are the process for organizing and mobilizing interest groups. Various states (e.g., New York), labor (e.g., the AFL-CIO and the NEA), women and other groups are organizing politically to further their own interest, hedging against a candidate who moves to lock up the nomination early, and against a brokered convention.

Blacks do not have enough influence in any of these other constituencies to trust their interest to anyone else. Thus, blacks and other rejected interest groups must create their own protection.

Let me emphasize that I am not urging blacks to pursue a *separatist* black agenda. What's good for black people is good for everybody with jobs, growth, and dignity for all, world peace and human rights. But what is perceived by some democrats to be good for them — a strategy along Jordan-Lance lines designed to allow them to squeak back into power in '84 — is not good for blacks.

Blacks now cast 20 percent of the national democratic vote, but they have not shared in the proprietorship of the party. Investors without equity are not guaranteed a share of the profits.

What would a successful black candidacy require? It requires the masses, machinery and money.

A black candidate must have the ability to galvanize the masses and to define, interpret, and defend the national interest generally, and the interests of black, non-white, poor and rejected people specifically.

A black candidate must also be able to attract adequate and broadly based financial support, although the ability to match the spending of other candidates would not be necessary. In Chicago, Jane Byrne raised $11 million, young Richard Daley raised four million, but Rep. Harold Washington — with less than one million in his campaign chest — defeated them both.

Washington's example in the recent Chicago primary is important in another way. He demonstrated the advantage of a united bloc of votes in a crowded field. Blacks represent 20 percent of the democratic electorate. If there are eight democratic candidates in 1984, any candidate who can gain 20 percent of the delegates would have tremendous influence at the convention. And a black candidate who builds the sort of coalition described above could well get that many delegates or more.

It is even more important that we make the case that a black candidate really could win. We certainly should not be defeated; it's not up to us to announce what we cannot do.

But the by-products of a black candidacy would justify the campaign. A credible and attractive candidacy would move the issues of social justice, war and peace, hurt and healing (at home and abroad) to the top of the national agenda. It would excite, maybe even electrify, the black, the young, the rejected and unrepresented masses, increasing their voter registration and political participation. For example, if black voter registration went from its current 10 million to 14 million, black participation could go from the seven million of 1980 to 14 million in 1984. This would have major ramifications for both blacks and the Democratic party; we're not even counting increased poor white, Hispanic, youth, or other voter registration that such a candidacy would surely stimulate.

An increase in voter registration and political participation would have a profound impact on the status quo of the Democratic party during the primaries, but it would also eventually have an impact on the Republican party and the nation in the general election. Eighteen million eligible and 12 to 14 million active black voters, inspired by live option, could not be ignored.

During the debates, blacks would no longer be in the *kitchen cabinet* passing notes from the trailer to the candidates on stage, but would be *on* the stage arguing the nation's agenda from a different perspective. Six to 10 new black congresspersons could be a by-product. Psychologically, it would help bring to an end ideas and feelings of black inferiority and white superiority. There are blacks capable of being president of the United States.

What are some of the objections? One is that a black candidacy would appeal only to black voters. Not true. A black candidate who advances the issues of concern to Hispanics, women, the poor, and whites who are interested in social justice, should be able to attract them too. Blacks have had experience with running and winning in areas that do not have majority black populations (for example, Tom Bradley as mayor of Los Angeles, and Alan Wheat and Ron Dellums as congressmen from Missouri and California, respectively). Clearly these victories could only have occurred because black candidates had community appeal.

Black leaders in other fields of endeavor have been able to attract more than just black support. In athletics, art, science, literature, and the media, blacks have pulled down curtains of resistance and operated beyond the ethnic domain. Now, in politics (and in corporate life) blacks must overcome the restraining forces and do the same.

There is no reason why a black presidential candidate who emphasizes an economy in crisis, massive unemployment, excessive concentrations of wealth, tax reform, war and peace, guns instead of butter — just to mention a few — would not have broad appeal. These are all general concerns of national importance which happen to overlap with particular interests of blacks.

Another argument has been that black candidacy would split the Democratic party and hurt the party's chances of regaining the White House in 1984. Some say a black candidacy will divide the South. Yet, no one points to former Florida Gov. Reuben Askew or South Carolina's Ernest Hollings — active or potential candidates who have a Southern base — and says that their campaigns are divisive.

The contention that a black candidacy would split the progressive forces and allow a candidate less sympathetic to the concerns of progressives to capture the nomination is not valid either.

Consider the examples of John F. Kennedy and Lyndon B. Johnson. Nominally, Kennedy was the more *liberal* but in the final analysis, Johnson turned out to be very supportive of blacks and the rejected. Johnson was not a static politician; he grew as the black vote and human rights struggle presented him with new political options.

On the other hand, in the recent Chicago mayoral primary, the two politicians in the Democratic party who are considered the most progressive, Walter F. Mondale and Edward M. Kennedy, not only failed to endorse and work for the most progressive candidate for mayor, Rep. Washington, but endorsed and worked for his opponents.

Moreover, their contempt, disrespect or disconnection from blacks and Hispanics was so great that they dived into a primary election in a city that is 42 percent black and 18 percent Hispanic without even consulting the three black congresspersons: State Comptroller Roland Burris, the largest vote-getter in the state in the November election; Richard Hatcher (in neighboring Gary, Ind.) the vice-chairperson and highest ranking black at the Democratic National Committee; or local and national black and Hispanic leaders.

Before 1965, when blacks and Hispanics had no political straps or boots, the suggestion to pick yourself up by your boot-straps was simply cruel. But now that 24 million blacks and Hispanics do have potential political straps and boots (with feet in them), they ought to lace them up and — for their own betterment, and for the enrichment of the entire nation — run.

# Johnson, Clark Plea for Third Party Presidential Presence for 1984

Citizens Voice, *San Francisco,*
*Sunday September 4, 1983*

*Citizens Party Convention Votes to Run*
*Presidential Candidate*
*142 in Favor    30 Against    1 Abstention*

"Now is the time for a woman to break the boring deadlock of presidential politics where look-alike white males drone on with sound-alike politics," stated Sonia Johnson.

Johnson, an ERA activist and housewife turned heretic, who challenged the force of the Mormon Church, is ready to challenge the force of entrenched male political tradition in the United States.

"The women's movement lacks a dream we can believe in," said Johnson. "We fear that the effort to get into the system will change us far more than we will change it."

Her long speech yesterday was a dramatic, emotional presentation that caught much of the audience up in her feminist appeal. As she moved into the more sensitive areas of women's anger against the effects of men's repression against women, she named the men in the audience 'honorary women'.

## Clark Concurs

Ramsey Clark, former-U.S. Attorney General, affirmed the need for a multi-party presence in the U.S., so that voters could have a choice of principles rather than just a choice of personalities.

"We have as much choice today as the Salvadoreans had a year ago." Clark charged. "They weren't going to get land reform from either side."

Clark supported the push for a Jesse Jackson campaign.

"I say, 'Run, Jess, run'. But I also say, 'Run, Citizens party, run!'"

## Commoner Proposes Coalition

Barry Commoner, the 1980 Citizens party candidate for president, told of events leading to his endorsement of Jesse Jackson, as reported in a recent article in the *New York Times*. When the executive committee had not acted upon his request to contact Jesse Jackson three months ago, Commoner became impatient. When Jackson appealed to him for support, Commoner said he made a decision to respond as an individual, not as a spokesperson for the Citizens party. "I talked to the *New York Times* because they called me up," he stated. "People think that when I speak, I speak for the Citizens party... Who am I? I'm just me... I've been humbled by being a member of the progressive left. I am no longer an elitist."

Commoner believes that Jackson's candidacy is a political development of the first magnitude, and that the Citizens party should join other progressives in a *Rainbow Coalition*. He pointed out that the poor and oppressed all over the world will respond to a candidate who is black and viable. The number of black voters who are unregistered equals the number of votes between Carter and Reagan, he remarked.

Members of the convention gave an enthusiastic response to Commoner when he said, "The Citizens party has two zingers for candidates!" (Johnson and Clark).

Commoner pleaded for unity in the party. "Conflict is unnecessary and unwarranted," he stated. "My position is different from what it was when I arrived at this convention." He urged delegates to join in the *Rainbow Coalition* (without formal endorsement of Jackson being necessary). At the same time, the party should talk about a presidential campaign of its own, he said.

# Reagan's Record Margin is 16,876,932 votes in the 1984 Presidential Election

## President's Popular Vote Lead Second Biggest in History, Official Tallies Show

WASHINGTON, Dec. 21, 1984 (AP) — President Reagan won re-election by almost 16.8 million votes, double his 1980 margin and the second-largest presidential victory in United States history, according to official results from all 50 states.

The certified tallies gathered from the state capitals showed Reagan, the republican candidate, with 54,450,603 votes to 37,573,671 for Walter F. Mondale, the democratic candidate, a difference of 16,876,932.

Reagan's re-election margin in the popular vote was exceeded only by Richard M. Nixon's 18 million vote victory over George McGovern in 1972.

Reagan carried every state except Mondale's home state, Minnesota — which he lost by 3,761 votes out of more than two million cast — and the District of Columbia. Reagan captured 525 electoral votes to Mondales's 13.

## Highest Electoral Count

That was the most electoral votes ever won, but Reagan's margin in the popular vote, 59 percent to 41 percent, ranked behind somewhat larger victories by Lyndon B. Johnson in 1964, Franklin D. Roosevelt in 1936, Nixon in 1972 and Warren G. Harding in 1920.

Reagan defeated President Carter in 1980 by a margin of 51 percent to 41 percent, winning 43.9 million votes to Carter's 35.5 million.

A dozen minor party or independent candidates got almost 600,000 votes this year, down sharply from the totals in the last four presidential elections. The total vote for such candidates in 1980 was more than 6.7 million; in 1976 it was about 1.6 million; in 1972, 1.3 million, and 1968, more than 10 million votes.

The leading third party candidate this year was the Libertarian party's David Bergland, who was on the ballot in 39 states and received 227,949 votes. Four years ago the libertarian candidate, Ed Clark, got 920,859 votes after waging a well-financed campaign.

Lyndon H. LaRouche Jr., the conservative who ran as an independent after also running in the democratic primaries, was next with 78,773 votes, followed by the feminist Sonia Johnson, who got 72,153 votes on the Citizens party line.

The turnout exceeded 92.6 million votes, six million more than in 1980. The figures include write-in votes reported by some states but not all.

Other independents with more than ten thousand votes were: Bob Richards, the Populist party candidate, a former Olympic pole vaulter, 62,371; Dennis Serrette of the Independent Alliance, 47,209; the Communist party leader, Gus Hall, 35,561; Mel Mason of the Social Workers party, 24,687; Larry Holmes of Workers World, 15,220; Delmar Dennis of the American party, 13,150, and Ed Winn of the Workers League, 10,801.

John B. Anderson, the former republican congressman from Illinois who got 5.7 million votes as an independent in 1980, ruled out a race this year and endorsed Mondale, but his name was on the ballot in Kentucky under the banner of the National Unity party of Kentucky. He got 1,479 votes.

Earl F. Dodge of the Prohibition party got 4,242 votes and Gavrielle Homes, a second Workers World candidate in some states, got 2,178.

In Nevada, voters had a chance to cast ballots for "none of the above," and 3,950 did. In Massachusetts, 35,601 people left their presidential ballots blank. New York officials reported that 194,108 ballots were blank, void or scattered among little-know candidates.

Reagan made a hastily scheduled campaign stop in Minnesota a few days before the Nov. 6 election when his aides realized that a 50-state sweep was within his grasp.

Mondale's victory, 1,036,364 to 1,032,603, was the closest presidential race in Minnesota since 1916, when Charles Evans Hughes, the republican candidate, carried the state by 392 votes over Woodrow Wilson.

# *Afterword*

The Citizens party had not scheduled a national convention to consider running a presidential slate in 1988, at the time this book went to press.

# APPENDIX

## APPENDIX I

### Citizens Party Platform

This update was made at the September 1983 convention in San Francisco.

These motions and amendments were offered and discussed at the convention but were either withdrawn or tabled.

*Environment and Resources:*

Amendment: by Missouri to add: Root causes of many of the problems facing us including pollution, nuclear war and other forms of violence, racism, and sexism, lie in not living in harmony with the environment, both the physical environment and all living things that are part of it. The Citizens party believes that both political and economic decision-making must occur within a framework dedicated to the promotion of ecological harmony. Specifically, it favors the creation of such programs as:

- Tax breaks for individuals and groups conserving nonrenewable resources while eliminating corporate tax subsidies which encourage the use of nonrenewable resources;
- Legislation promoting a decentralized, sustainable food system, with the creation of seed banks to preserve genetic diversity in agriculture;
- Policies which demand that all programs using public money are in harmony with ecological principles;
- Policies which demand that corporate decision-making

cannot violate ecological principles. The motion is seconded.

Amendment: to be added as a last point: Surtaxes to be imposed
on those factories and industries, and slum landlords who contribute
to pollution. The amendment is not accepted as friendly.

There is objection to the entire motion on the grounds that it is
too sketchy and will need a rewrite at a later date. Missouri withdraws
the motion.

Amendment: by the Vermont delegation to Evergreen:
We support the conversion to publicly-owned and operated
business, various industries and sectors, specifically the energy,
railroad and mass transit, utilities, banking and insurance industries.
The motion is seconded.

There is a simultaneous motion then proposed by Virginia,
relevant to Economic Policy, A#1, to be replaced with the following:

Motion: The Citizens party proposes to transform all large
corporations into public, democratically-managed entities, whose
purpose in society is not to earn profits, but to provide public services
for the satisfaction of human needs and to replace the opening of #2
to read, "Public management for public service would include."

The parliamentarian ruled that the Virginia motion does not deal
with the Vermont motion, therefore they are not simultaneous. We
return to the Vermont motion. Massachussetts speaks against deleting
the last sentence. Vermont accepts leaving that sentence in: Public
ownership should be implemented at the least centralized level
feasible and in such a way as to make the industry more accountable
to the public.

Minnesota proposes a simultaneous motion to amend section A,
sentence one to read:

Motion: The Citizens party proposes to place corporations above
a specified size under public control.

The chair recognizes that discussion time has elapsed and suggests we vote on these as simultaneous motions ending the session.

Point of Procedure: That when the body voted on limiting discussion to 15 minutes per section, if we weren't able to come to clear agreement at the end of 15 minutes, we would table it and deal with it at another time. Since this is a discussion of a substantive, complex issue, table it and work on it later.

Motion: To table the amendments. No debate. The question is called and the motion to table is carried by voice vote.

# Barry Commoner Fact Sheet

Born
May 28, 1917, Brooklyn, New York

Education

| | |
|---|---|
| A.B., Columbia College (with honors in Zoology) | 1937 |
| M.A., Harvard University (Biology) | 1938 |
| Ph.D., Harvard University (Biology) | 1941 |

Military Service

| | |
|---|---|
| U.S. Naval Air Force | 1942-1946 |

Academic Career

| | |
|---|---|
| 1947-1953 | Associate Professor of Plant Physiology, Washington University, St. Louis. |
| 1953-1976 | Professor of Plant Physiology, Washington University, St. Louis. |
| 1965 | Director, Center for the Biology of Natural Systems, Washington University, St. Louis. |
| 1976 | University Professor of Environmental Science, Washington University, St. Louis. |

Positions (partial listing)

| | |
|---|---|
| 1963-1979 | Board of Directors, Scientists Institute for Public Information |
| 1958-1965 | Chairman, Committee on Science in the Promotion of Human Welfare, American Association for the Advancement of Science. |
| 1967-1974 | Board of Directors, American Association for the Advancement of Science. |
| 1969-1974 | Chairman, AAAS Committee on Environmental Alterations. |

Books
1966    *Science and Survival*, New York, The Viking Press.
1971    *The Closing Circle*, New York, Alfred A. Knopf, Inc.
1973    *La Technologia del Profitto*, Rome, Editori Riuniti.
1976    *The Poverty of Power*, New York, Alfred A. Knopf, Inc.
1976    *Ecologia e Lotte Sociali*, With Virginio Bettini, Milan, Feltrinelli.
1979    *The Politics of Energy*, New York, Alfred A. Knopf, Inc.

# Popular Vote Totals in the 1980 Presidential Election

| | | | | | | |
|---|---|---|---|---|---|---|
| Ronald Reagan | (CA) | Republican | 69 | Ex-Governor | 43,904,153 | 50.75 |
| Jimmy Carter | (GA) | Democrat | 56 | President | 35,483,883 | 41.02 |

**INDEPENDENT**

| | | | | | | |
|---|---|---|---|---|---|---|
| John Anderson | (IL) | National Unity | 58 | Congressman | 5,720,060 | 6.61 |

**THIRD PARTIES**

| | | | | | | |
|---|---|---|---|---|---|---|
| Edward Clark | (CA) | Libertarian | 50 | Attorney | 921,299 | 1.06 |
| Barry Commoner | (NY) | Citizens | 63 | Professor | 234,294 | 0.27 |
| Andrew Pulley | (IL) | Socialist Workers | 29 | Steelworker | 49,038 | 0.05 |

(Plus DeBarry and Richard Congress)          (Combined Total)

| | | | | | | |
|---|---|---|---|---|---|---|
| Gus Hall | (NY) | Communist | 70 | Party Official | 45,023 | 0.05 |
| John Rarick | (LA) | Amer. Independ. | 56 | Ex-Congressman | 41,268 | 0.05 |
| Ellen McCormack | (NY) | Right to Life | 54 | Homemaker | 32,327 | 0.04 |
| Deirdre Griswold | (NJ) | Workers World | 44 | Editor | 13,300 | 0.02 |
| Benjamin Bubar | (ME) | Prohibition | 63 | Baptist Minister | 7,212 | 0.01 |

(National Statesman)

| | | | | | | |
|---|---|---|---|---|---|---|
| D. McReynolds | (NY) | Socialist | 50 | Antiwar Activist | 6,898 | 0.01 |
| Percy Greaves | (NY) | American | 74 | Economist | 6,647 | 0.01 |
| Write-Ins and Miscellaneous* | | | | | 43,223 | 0.05 |

---

* Margaret Smith received 18,116 votes as the Peace and Freedom party candidate in California but she ran in only one state. Other miscellaneous and write-in votes were cast for Kurt Lynen, middle-class candidate, (3,694); Bill Gahres, Dow With Lawyers (1,718); Frank Shelton, American (1,555); Martin Wendalken, Independent (923); Harley McLain, National Peoples League (296); and write-ins (16,921).

# *Petition Requirements for the 1980 Presidential Election*

| STATE | ELECTORAL VOTE | CRITERIA | ESTIMATED SIGNATURES REQUIRED | CANDIDATES ON BALLOT |
|---|---|---|---|---|
| GROUP ONE (States requiring 25,000 or more petition signatures) | | | | |
| California | (45) | 1% of Registered Voters | 101,000+ | 7 |
| Georgia | (12) | 5% of Eligible Voters | 57,000+ | 4 |
| Maryland | (10) | 3% of Registered Voters | 55,000+ | 4 |
| Pennsylvania | (27) | 2% of Largest Prev. Statewide Vote | 48,000+ | 7 |
| Florida | (17) | 1% of Registered Voters | 42,000+ | 4 |
| Massachusetts | (14) | 2% Previous Governor's Vote | 39,000+ | 5 |
| Oklahoma | ( 8) | 3% Previous Presidential Vote | 33,000+ | 4 |
| Oregon | ( 6) | 3% Previous Presidential Vote | 30,000+ | 5 |
| Michigan | (21) | 1% Previous Secretary of State | 28,000 | 6 |
| Illinois | (26) | Specified Minimum Requirement | 25,000 | 8 |

SUMMARY:   Total Number of States:                          10
              Total Electoral College Votes:              186
              Average Signature Requirement:        45,900
              Average Candidates on Ballot:              5.4

| STATE | ELECTORAL VOTE | CRITERIA | ESTIMATED SIGNATURES REQUIRED | CANDIDATES ON BALLOT |
|---|---|---|---|---|
| GROUP TWO (States requiring 1,000 or fewer petition signatures) | | | | |
| Washington | ( 9) | 1 Signature/10,000 Presidential Votes | 155 | 9 |
| Tennessee | (10) | 25 Electors in 10 Congressional Districts | 250 | 10 |
| North Dakota | ( 3) | Specified Minimum Requirement | 300 | 10 |
| Utah | ( 4) | Specified Minimum Requirement | 500 | 9 |
| New Jersey | (17) | Specified Minimum Requirement | 800 | 11 |
| Iowa | ( 8) | Specified Minimum Requirement | 1,000 | 10 |
| New Hmpsh. | ( 4) | Specified Minimum Requirement | 1,000 | 8 |
| Vermont | ( 3) | Specified Minimum Requirement | 1,000 | 8 |

| STATE | ELECTORAL VOTE | CRITERIA | ESTIMATED SIGNATURES REQUIRED | CANDIDATES ON BALLOT |
|---|---|---|---|---|
| Rhode Island | ( 4) | Specified Minimum Requirement | 1,000 | 8 |
| Mississippi | ( 7) | Specified Minimum Requirement | 1,000 | 6 |

SUMMARY:

| | | |
|---|---|---|
| Total Number of States: | 10 |
| Total Electoral College Votes: | 69 |
| Average Signature Requirement: | 700 |
| Average Candidates on Ballot: | 8.8 |

# Popular Vote Totals in the 1984 Presidential Election

Certified totals for Ronald Reagan, Walter F. Mondale and other top finishers: David Bergland, Libertarian; Lyndon H. LaRouche Jr., Independent, and Sonia Johnson, Citizens party. Figures include some write-in votes.

|  | Reagan Republican | Mondale Democrat | Bergland Libertarian | LaRouche Independent | Johnson Citizens |
|---|---|---|---|---|---|
| Ala. | 872,849 | 551,899 | 9,504 |  |  |
| Alaska | 138,392 | 62,018 | 6,378 |  |  |
| Ariz. | 681,416 | 333,584 | 10,585 |  | 18 |
| Ark. | 534,774 | 338,646 | 2,221 | 1,890 | 960 |
| Calif. | 5,467,009 | 3,922,519 | 49,951 |  | 26,297 |
| Colo. | 821,817 | 454,975 | 11,257 | 4,662 | 23 |
| Conn. | 890,877 | 569,597 |  |  |  |
| Del. | 152,190 | 101,656 | 268 | 121 |  |
| D.C. | 29,009 | 180,408 | 279 | 127 |  |
| Fla. | 2,730,350 | 1,448,816 | 754 |  | 58 |
| Ga. | 1,068,722 | 706,628 |  |  |  |
| Hawaii | 185,050 | 147,154 | 2,167 | 654 |  |
| Idaho | 297,523 | 108,510 | 2,823 |  |  |
| Ill. | 2,707,103 | 2,086,499 | 10,086 |  | 2,716 |
| Ind. | 1,377,230 | 841,481 | 6,741 |  |  |
| Iowa | 703,088 | 605,620 | 1,844 | 6,248 |  |
| Kan. | 677,296 | 333,149 | 3,329 |  |  |
| Ky. | 821,702 | 539,539 |  | 1,766 | 599 |
| La. | 1,037,299 | 651,586 | 1,876 | 3,552 | 9,502 |
| Me. | 336,500 | 214,515 |  |  |  |
| Md. | 879,918 | 787,935 | 5,712 |  |  |
| Mass. | 1,310,936 | 1,239,606 | 2 |  | 18 |
| Mich. | 2,251,571 | 1,529,638 | 10,055 | 3,862 | 1,191 |

|        | Reagan Republican | Mondale Democrat | Bergland Libertarian | LaRouche Independent | Johnson Citizens |
|--------|-------------------|------------------|----------------------|----------------------|------------------|
| Minn.  | 1,032,603         | 1,036,364        | 2,996                | 3,865                | 1,219            |
| Miss.  | 582,377           | 352,192          | 2,336                | 1,001                |                  |
| Mo.    | 1,274,188         | 848,583          |                      |                      | 2                |
| Mont.  | 232,450           | 146,742          | 5,185                |                      |                  |
| Neb.   | 459,135           | 187,475          | 2,075                |                      |                  |
| Nev.   | 188,770           | 91,655           | 2,292                |                      |                  |
| N.H.   | 267,050           | 120,347          | 735                  | 467                  |                  |
| N.J.   | 1,933,630         | 1,261,323        | 6,416                |                      | 1,247            |
| N.M.   | 307,101           | 201,769          | 4,459                |                      | 455              |
| N.Y.   | 3,664,763         | 3,119,605        | 11,949               |                      |                  |
| N.C.   | 1,346,481         | 824,287          | 3,794                |                      |                  |
| N.D.   | 200,336           | 104,429          | 703                  | 1,278                | 368              |
| Ohio   | 2,678,560         | 1,825,440        | 5,886                | 10,693               |                  |
| Okla.  | 861,530           | 385,080          | 9,066                |                      |                  |
| Ore    | 685,700           | 536,479          |                      |                      |                  |
| Pa.    | 2,584,323         | 2,228,131        | 6,982                |                      | 21,628           |
| R.I    | 208,513           | 194,294          | 241                  |                      | 211              |
| S.C.   | 615,539           | 344,459          | 4,359                |                      |                  |
| S.D.   | 200,267           | 116,113          |                      |                      |                  |
| Tenn.  | 990,212           | 711,714          | 3,072                | 1,852                | 967              |
| Tex.   | 3,433,428         | 1,949,276        | 14,613               |                      | 87               |
| Utah   | 469,105           | 155,369          | 2,447                |                      | 844              |
| Vt.    | 135,865           | 95,730           | 1,002                | 423                  | 264              |
| Va.    | 1,337,078         | 796,250          |                      | 12,307               |                  |
| Wash.  | 1,051,670         | 807,352          | 8,884                | 4,712                | 1,891            |
| W.Va.  | 405,483           | 328,125          |                      |                      |                  |
| Wis.   | 1,198,548         | 995,740          | 4,883                | 3,791                | 1,456            |
| Wyo.   | 133,241           | 53,370           | 2,357                |                      |                  |
| TOTALS | 54,450,603        | 37,573,671       | 227,949              | 78,773               | 72,153           |

# Citizens Party Electoral History

## 1980
Presidential Campaign: Barry Commoner & LaDonna Harris: On the ballot in 30 states, a 20th century first for a new party; 234, 294 votes cast for ticket.

38 Campaigns, 11 States. Highlights:

| | | | | |
|---|---|---|---|---|
| Richard Stafford | Lakeville, MA | Finance Comm | | Victory |
| Robin Lloyd | Vermont | US Congress | 13% | |
| Max Weiner | Pennsylvania | US Congress | 10% | |
| Terry Bouricius | Vermont | State Legislature | 21% | |
| Robert Swearingen | Missouri | State Legislature | 15% | |

## 1981
58 Campaigns, 14 States. Highlights:

| | | | | |
|---|---|---|---|---|
| Terry Bouricius | Burlington VT | City Council | 52% | Victory |
| Carolyn Micklas | Schenectady NY | School Board | 26% | Victory |
| Michael Preston | Seattle WA | School Board | 69% | Victory |
| John Swet | Atlanta GA | City Council | 49% | |
| Greg Guma | Burlington VT | City Council | 41% | |
| Fred Perez | New Haven CT | City Council | 30% | |
| Bob Cohen | Albany NY | City Council | 29% | |
| Harriet Sallach | Columbia MO | City Council | 26% | |

## 1982
Spring; 29 Campaigns, 3 States. Highlights:

| | | | | |
|---|---|---|---|---|
| Zoe Breiner | Burlington VT | City Council | 51% | Victory |
| Rick Musty | Burlington VT | City Council | 48% | Victory |
| Stanton Kahn | Portland OR | Metro Srvc Dist | 47% | Victory |

Fall; 80 Campaigns, 20 States. Highlights

| | | | | |
|---|---|---|---|---|
| Julie Hand | Burlington VT | Insptr/elections | 18% | Victory |
| Michele Weiss | Burlington VT | Insptr/elections | 17% | Victory |
| J. Bear Baker | Denver CO | Reg. Trans. Cncl | 37% | Victory |
| Renee Zella | Denver CO | Reg. Trans. Cncl | 22% | |
| Bob Klein | Athens GA | City Council | 34% | |
| Jon Seawright | Athens GA | City Council | 18% | |
| Greg Jocoy | Athens GA | State Assembly | 20% | |
| Danny Feig | Atlanta GA | State Senate | 19% | |
| Larry Beeferman | Cambridge MA | State Assembly | 17% | |
| Laurel Paulson | Eugene OR | State Assembly | 21% | |
| Janet Stuart | Yamhill OR | County Clerk | 26% | |
| Dolores Tucker | Philadelphia PA | State Senate | 15% | |
| Tim McKenzie | Burlington VT | State Assembly | 33% | |
| Arthur Stone | LoMoille CO VT | State Senate | 45% | |
| Judith Ashkenaz | Windham CO VT | State Senate | 15% | |
| Wayne Grytting | Seattle WA | State Assembly | 16% | |

1983
6 Campaigns, 2 States. Highlights:

| | | | | |
|---|---|---|---|---|
| Elliot Lefko | Houston TX | Citizens Participation Comm. | | Victory |
| Terry Bouricius | Burlington VT | City Council | 60% | Victory |
| Peter Lackowski | Burlington VT | City Council | 60% | Victory |
| Nancy Margolin | Burlington VT | Insptr/ Elections | | Victory |

# 1983 Campaigns

| | | |
|---|---|---|
| Iowa City, IA | City Council | James Schwab |
| Des Moines, IA | City Council | Robert Willis |
| | | |
| Indianapolis, IN | City-County Council | Fred Widlak |
| Indianapolis, IN | City-County Council | David Duvall |
| Indianapolis, IN | City-County Council | Jane Haldeman |
| Indianapolis, IN | City-County Council | Altha Cravey |
| Indianapolis, IN | City-County Council | Sheila Adsit |
| Bloomington, IN | City Council | Pete Tescione |
| Bloomington, IN | City Clerk | Jim Hurd |
| Bloomington, IN | City Council | Jim Simmons |
| Bloomington, IN | City Council | Bob Decker |
| Bloomington, IN | City Council | Mitchell Rice |
| Bloomington, IN | City Council | Paul Swaine |
| | | |
| St. Paul, MN | City Council | Paul Hildebrant |
| St. Paul, MN | City Council | Irv Sutley |
| St. Paul, MN | City Council | David Horton |
| Minneapolis, MN | City Council | Kristine Gronquist |
| Minneapolis, MN | City Council | Marshall Helmberger |
| Minneapolis, MN | City Council | Jane Seeman |
| Minneapolis, MN | City Council | Robert Halfhill |
| Minneapolis, MN | City Council | Lloyd Hansen |
| Minneapolis, MN | City Council | Phil Kashian |
| Minneapolis, MN | Alderman (incumbent) | Kathy O'Brien |
| Minneapolis, MN | School Board | David Tilsen |
| | | |
| Ocean County, NJ | General Assembly | John Kinnevy III |
| | | |
| Albany, NY | County Legislature | Sharon Gonsalezes |
| Albany, NY | County Legislature | Lorraine Freeman |
| Ithaca, NY | City Council | Kirby Edmonds |
| New Paltz, NY | Town Council | Glenn Gidaly |
| New Paltz, NY | Ulster Cty Legislature | Tim Stephens |

| | | |
|---|---|---|
| New Paltz, NY | Ulster Cty Legislature | Maurice Recchia |
| Schenectady, NY | City Council | Kate Skelton-Caban |
| Schenectady, NY | City Council | Victor Caban |
| Schenectady, NY | City Council | Esther Willison |
| Schenectady, NY | City Council | Judith Antokol |
| Schenectady, NY | City Council | Angela Nelligan |
| Syracuse, NY | City Council | Garnell Gladden |
| Syracuse, NY | Onodaga Cty Legislature | Wayne Hall |
| | | |
| Aberlmarle Co, VA | Cty Bd of Supervisors | James Duffer |
| Richmond VA | County of Legislature | Earl Chandler |

# APPENDIX II

*Notice: This opinion is subject to formal revision before publication in the Federal Reporter or U.S.App.D.C. Reports. Users are requested to notify the Clerk of any formal errors in order that corrections may be made before the bound volumes go to press.*

*UNITED STATES COURT OF APPEALS
FOR THE DISTRICT OF COLUMBIA CIRCUIT*

*No. 84-1508*

*SONIA JOHNSON and RICHARD WALTON, PETITIONERS*

*v.*

*FEDERAL COMMUNICATIONS COMMISSION and
UNITED STATES of AMERICA, RESPONDENTS*

*NATIONAL BROADCASTING COMPANY, INC.
CBS, Inc.,
AMERICAN BROADCASTING COMPANIES, Inc., INTERVENORS*

*Petition for Review of an Order of the
Federal Communications Commission*

*Argued October 21, 1985
Decided September 22, 1987*

*John C. Armor* for petitioners.

*C. Grey Pash, Jr.,* Counsel, Federal Communications Commission, with whom *J. Paul McGrath,* Assistant Attorney General, *Jack D. Smith,* General Counsel, *Daniel M. Armstrong,* Associate General Counsel, Federal Communications Commission, *Andrea Limmer* and *Catherine G. O'Sullivan,* Attorneys, Department of Justice, were on the brief, for respondents.

*Joseph DeFranco, John W. Zucker* and *Howard Monderer* were on the brief for intervenors, CBS, Inc., and NBC, Inc.

*Carl R. Ramey* entered an appearance for intervenor American Broadcasting Companies, Inc.

Before ROBINSON, EDWARDS and SCALIA*, *Circuit Judges.*
Opinion for the Court filed by *Circuit Judge* Robinson.

ROBINSON, *Circuit Judge:* In 1984, feminist-activist Sonia Johnson ran for President as the nominee of the Citizens party. Richard Walton, a Citizens party founder and foreign policy author, campaigned as her running mate. Ultimately, they qualified for the ballot in nineteen states, and finished fifth in the election with .08 percent of the vote.[1]

On July 24, 1984, Johnson and Walton wrote a series of letters to the League of Women Voters, the three major private networks, and the Public Broadcasting System, requesting inclusion in the League of Women Voters' presidential and vice-presidential debates scheduled for and conducted in the fall of that year.[2] On August 15, they filed a complaint with the Federal Communications Commission against the networks, the Democratic and Republican National

---

* Judge (now Justice) Scalia was a member of the panel at the time this case was argued, but did not participate in this opinion.

[1] Joint Brief for Intervenors CBS, Inc., and National Broadcasting Company, Inc. [hereinafter Brief for Intervenors] at 16-17.

[2] Appendix for Respondent (R. App.) 24-28. On August 30, the request was denied by the League of Women Voters, sponsors of the debate. R. App. 41.

Committees, the major party candidates, and the League, asserting upcoming violation of the Communications Act[3] and the First Amendment,[4] and seeking an order that would prohibit the televising of any debate from which they were excluded.[5] The Commission's staff denied the complaint on October 4, 1984;[6] the Commission rejected an application for review of the staff ruling a day later.[7] This petition for review followed.

## I. THE PARTIES' CONTENTIONS

Petitioners claim that by 1984 the televised presidential and vice-presidential debates had become so institutionalized as to be a prerequisite for election. If this is the case, they argue, then their exclusion from the 1984 debates would restrict their access to the ballot and impinge upon associated choices protected by the First

---

[3] 47 U.S.C.sec 151-611 (1982).

[4] U.S. Const. amend. 1

[5] Appendix for Petitioner (P. App.) E-1, E-5.

[6] *Sonia Johnson and Richard Walton*, No. 8330-B, C8-405 (Mass Media Bureau, Oct 4, 1984) (staff ruling), *reprinted in* 56 Rad. Reg. 2d(P & F) at 1534 (Oct. 4, 1984).

[7] *Sonia Johnson and Richard Walton*, F.C.C. Docket No. 84-478, 56 Rad. Reg. 2d (P & F) 1533 (Oct. 5, 1984).

Even though the 1984 election is now over, no one has suggested that the case is moot, and we are satisfied that it is not. The issues properly presented, and their effects on minor-party candidacies, will persist in future elections, and within a time frame too short to allow resolution through litigation. This is, therefore, a case where the controversy is "capable of repetition, yet evading review," *Storer v. Brown*, 415 U.S. 725, 737 n.8, 94 S.Ct. 1274, 1282 n.8, 39 L.Ed.2d 714, 727 n.8 (1974) (*quoting Southern Pac. Terminal Co.v.ICC,*219 U.S. 498,515,31 S. Ct. 279, 283, 55 L.Ed. 310, 316(1911)). Accord *Anderson v. Celebrezze*, 460 U.S. 780, 784 n.3, 103 S.Ct. 1564, 1567 n.3, 75 L.Ed.2d 547, 554 n.3 (1983), and as such may be decided now.

Amendment. Petitioners cite *Terry v. Adams*[8] and *Anderson v. Celebrezze*[9] as instances in which the Supreme Court has struck down action by governmental officials or private individuals that operated to foreclose the political opportunities of candidates and voters. The Commission and intervenors, on the other hand, assert first that there exists insufficient governmental action to establish the predicate for a constitutional violation,[10] and second, that decision by the Supreme

---

[8] 345 U.S. 461, 469-470, 73 S.Ct.809,813-814, 97 L.Ed.2d 1152, 1160-1161 (1953) (declaring racially exclusionary primary to be violative of the Fifteenth Amendment).

[9] 460 U.S. at 790-795, 103 S.Ct. at 1570-1573, 75 L.Ed.2d at 558-562 (striking down early filing deadline as a restriction on ballot access violative of the First Amendment).

[10] Brief for Respondents at 24-25; Brief for Intervenors at 5-11. Because we ultimately conclude that petitioners possessed no substantive First Amendment right to be included in the 1984 presidential and vice-presidential debates, we need not determine whether their exclusion by the broadcasters constituted governmental action for First Amendment purposes. See *Ripon Soc'y* v. *National Republican Party*, 173 U.S.App.D.C.350,361 n.28, 525 F.2d 567, 578 n.28 (1975). In *Business Executives' Move for Vietnam Peace* v. *FCC*, 146 U.S.App.D.C. 181, 188-191, 450 F.2d 642,649-654 (1971), this court characterized broadcasters' denial of access for political editorial advertisements as governmental action. The Supreme Court reversed *Business Executives'* on the question of whether the broadcasters substantively violated the First Amendment, but found it unnecessary to resolve the governmental-action question, over which it divided. *Columbia Broadcasting Sys.* v. *Democratic Nat'l Comm.*, 412 U.S. 94,114-121,93 S.Ct. 2080,2092-2096,36 L.Ed.2d 772,790-794(1973) (plurality opinion finding no governmental action);*id.* at 139-141, 93 S.Ct. at 2104-2105, 36 L.Ed.2d at 804-806(concurring opinion finding no govern-mental action); *id.*at146-148,93 S.Ct. at 2108-2109,36 L.Ed.2d at 809 (concurring opinions declining to reach question of govern-mental action);*id.* at 148-170, 93 S.Ct. at 2109-2120, 36 L.Ed.2d at 809-822 (concurring opinion finding no governmental action); *id.* at 172-182, 93 S.Ct. at 2122-2126, 36 L.Ed.2d at 823-829 (dissenting opinion finding governmental action). Our sister circuits have generally rejected claims that broadcasters

Court and this court on claims to broadcast access under the Communications Act and the First Amendment are dispositive of petitioners' contentions.[11]

In considering petitioners' claim, we must remain mindful of the regulatory framework that has evolved under the Communications Act and the decisions evaluating the broadcast-access provisions of the Act. Petitioners' argument essentially boils down to a demand for broadcast access, and access claims based upon various constitutional and statutory theories have been heard by the Supreme Court and this court on a number of occasions.[12] The broadcasting industry stands in a unique relationship to the First Amendment; its tremendous power to inform and shape public opinion and the immutable scarcity of broadcast frequencies have created both tremendous opportunities and serious hazards for free expression. The broadcast-access decisions of the Supreme Court and this court have analyzed comprehensively the many competing First Amendment interests affected by disputes over the control of and access to the airways. Congress, and the Commission acting under congressional authority, have responded by crafting an extensive system of government regulation that balances the potentially conflicting speech interests of individuals, broadcasters, and the general public.

We therefore first examine petitioners' arguments in the light of prior cases dealing with First Amendment access claims and the

---

action, at least absent the specific Commission approval here present, qualifies as state action. See, e.g., *Massachusetts Universalist Convention* v. *Hildreth & Rogers,* 183 F.2d 497, 501 (1st Cir. 1950); *Kuczo* v. *Western Conn. Broadcasting Co.,* 566 F.2d 384, 387-388 (2d Cir. 1977); *McIntire* v. *William Penn Broadcasting Co.,* 151,601 (3rd Cir. 1945); *Belluso* v. *Turner,* 633 F.2d 393,398-400 (5th Cir. 1980). Following the Supreme Court's lead on this thorny issue, we do not resolve it here.

[11] See Brief for Respondents at 17-24; Brief for Intervenors at 12-17.

[12] See, e.g., *Columbia Broadcasting Sys.* v. *Democratic Nat'l Comm., supra* note 10;*Red Lion Broadcasting Co.* v. FCC,395 U.S. 367, 89 S.Ct. 1794,23 L.Ed.2s 371(1969); *Kennedy for President Comm.*(Kennedy I) v. *FCC,* 204 U.S.App.D.C. 145,636 F.2d 417(1980); *Chisholm* v. *FCC,* 176 U.S.App.D.C. 1,538 F.2d 349 (1976).

Communications Act. We conclude that the Commission properly determined that petitioners had no right recognized by the Communications Act or the broadcast-access precedents to be in-cluded in the televised debates. We then proceed to determine whether the contentions petitioners base upon the ballot-access cases resolved under the First and Fifteenth Amendments raise significant First Amendment issues not adjudicated in earlier decisions. We find that petitioners have failed to show any intrusion upon the electoral process that would require the grant to them of access privileges beyond those conferred by the Communications Act. We therefore affirm the Commission's order.

## II. THE COMMUNICATIONS ACT AND THE FIRST AMENDMENT

In *Columbia Broadcasting System* v. *Democratic National Committee*,[13] the Supreme Court upheld a ban on editorial advertising imposed by broadcast licensees, rejecting fairness doctrine and First Amendment challenges. The Court held that claims of First Amendment rights to broadcast access must be examined in light of the regulatory scheme evolved from the Communications Act:

> Balancing the various First Amendment interests involved in the broadcast media and determining what best serves the public's right to be informed is a task of great delicacy and difficulty. The process must necessarily be undertaken within the framework of the regulatory scheme that has evolved over the course of the past half century. For, during that time, Congress and its chosen regulatory agency have established a delicately balanced system of regulations intended to serve the interests of all concerned.[14]

---

[13] *Supra* note 10.
[14] 412 U.S. at 102, 93 S.Ct.at2086,36 L.Ed.2d at 783.

The Court thus recognized that both broadcasters and the public have important First Amendment interests at stake in controversies over broadcast access. The Court concluded that Congress, by denying the public an unlimited right of access in the Communications Act, and the Commission, in developing the fairness doctrine, had attempted to strike a balance that would satisfy the First Amendment interests of all concerned.[15] While the Court acknowledged that it could not "defer" to the judgment of Congress or the Commission on a constitutional question,[16] it realized that contests over access oftimes present complex problems and few known answers, and that courts ought to pay careful attention to how the other branches of government have treated the same problem.[17]

We face a far more pervasive scheme of regulation, and a significantly greater congressional sensitivity when, as here, the First Amendment rights of candidates for public office and their supporters are involved. There is, accordingly, a particularly strong obligation to consider petitioners' claim of a right of access to the broadcast media against the backdrop of the balance of First Amendment interests embodied in the Communications Act, the policies of the Commission, and the caselaw. Candidates are accorded greater access to the broadcast media than other citizens; they are afforded not only a limited privilege of reasonable access[18] but also the right to match any nonexempt use of a broadcasting station by their opponents,[19] and freedom to purchase advertising space at the lowest available rate.[20] These statutory rights of access make clear that Congress intended a wide variety of political views to reach the general public during the course of an election campaign.

In a case not involving the broadcast media, the Supreme Court declared that "the primary values of the First Amendment... are

---

[15] *Id.* at 102,110-114, 93 S.Ct.at2086,2090-2092,36 L.Ed. 2d at 783, 788-790..

[16] *Id*, at 103,93 S.Ct. at 2087,36 L.Ed.2d at 784

[17] *Id.*

[18] 47 U.S.C. sec.312(a)(7) (1982); *Columbia Broadcasting Sys.* v. *FCC, supra* note 12,453 U.S. at 396,101 S.Ct. at 2830,69 L.Ed.2d at 729.

[19] 47 U.S.C. sec 315(a) (1982).

[20] 47 U.S.C. sec 315(b) (1982).

served when election campaigns are not monopolized by the existing political parties. "[21] Petitioners' claims rest in part upon fear that the voices of minor party candidates may be drowned out by the superior financial resources of the major parties, or encounter discrimination from conscious or unconscious biases of large broadcasters. However, the several access provisions of the Communications Act ensure that political debate will not be monopolized by one or a very few candidates, but that candidates from all points of the political spectrum will be able to utilize the media.[22]

While the Communications act thus affords candidates several avenues by which to gain television exposure, the televising of a debate sponsored by a non-network third party does not itself trigger access for competing candidates under the provisions of the Act. This is because the Commission, in a decision upheld by this court in Chisholm v. FCC, [23] has determined that debates between qualified political candidates initiated by nonbroadcast entities are exempt from the equal-time requirements of Section 315(a) of the Act.[24] In that case, we found nothing in the Commission's decision inconsistent with the basic philosophy of Section 315(a) as amended by Congress.[25] We concluded that Congress, in crafting the exceptions to the equal-time rule of Section 315(a), intended that the Commission play

---

[21] *Anderson* v. *Celebrezze, supra* note 7, 460 U.S. at 794,103 S.Ct. at 1573,75 L.Ed.2d at 561.

[22] This point may be illustrated by comparing the limited nature of access to electronic campaigning and the lack of regulated access to campaigning by print. Even if endorsement by prominent newspaper were shown to correlate mathematically to electoral success, the First Amendment not only would not assure access to this successful campaigning forum, but would forbid such an access requirement. See *Miami Herald Publishing Co.* v. *Tornillo,* 418 U.S. 241,94 S.Ct. 2831, 41 L.Ed.2d 730 (1974); see also *FCC* v. *League of Women Voters,* 468 U.S. 364,376,104 S.Ct. 3106,3115,82 L.Ed.2d 278,289 (1984).

[23] *Supra* note 12.

[24] 47 U.S.C. sec 315(a) (1982).

[25] See 176 U.S.App.D.C.at 18,538 F.2d at 366.

a large role in fine-tuning the Section 315(a) exemptions.[26] By casting the exemptions in terms of broad categories, Congress knowingly accepted the risk of broadcaster favoritism in order to promote wider coverage of political news.[27]

The *Chisholm* petitioners did not attack the Commission's Section 315(a) policy on First Amendment grounds. That challenge was made in this court in *Kennedy I*.[28] The question there was whether the legislative scheme embodied in Section 315(a) "transgress[ed] the First Amendment interest of a candidate demanding an opportunity to respond to another candidate's statements on an excepted occasion."[29] We felt then, as we do now, that the answer was evident. We read the Supreme Court's decision in *Columbia Broadcasting System* v. *Democratic National Committee* as a holding that "'no individual member of the public [has a right] to broadcast his own particular views on any matter.'"[30] Congress, we noted, has chosen to protect the public's First Amendments rights in broadcasting "by relying on broadcasters as public trustees, periodically accountable for their stewardship, to use their discretion in ensuring the public's access to conflicting ideas."[31] The Supreme Court had found in *Columbia Broadcasting System*, we said, that the congressional choice of a public trustee system over a system in which everyone had access to the media was reasonable in view of the scarcity of broadcast frequencies.

We can perceive no basis upon which to distinguish the case at bar from *Columbia Broadcasting System* and *Kennedy I.* Indeed,

---

[26] *Id.* at 9, 538 F.2d at 357.

[27] *Id.* at 18, 538 F. 2d at 366.

[28] *Supra* note 12.

[29] 204 U.S.App.D.C. at 160,636 F.2d at 432.

[30] *Id.*, 636 F.2d at 432 (quoting *Columbia Broadcasting Sys.* v. *Democratic Nat'l Comm.*, *supra* note 10, 412 U.S. at 112-113, 93 S.Ct. at 2091,36 L.Ed.2d at 789) (citation omitted).

[31] *Kennedy I, supra* note 12,204 U.S.App.D.C. at 160, 636 F.2d at 432 (*quoting Red Lion Broadcasting Co.* v. *FCC, supra* note 12,395 U.S. at 390, 89 S.Ct. at 1806,23 L.Ed.2d at 389)).

petitioners present a far weaker constitutional thesis than the ones those cases rejected. They seek, not general access, as in the former, nor an opportunity to respond to a particular broadcast, as in the latter, but rather the specific right to appear on a specific program— a program not organized by the broadcasters, but by a third party. Thus, viewed in light of the First Amendment balance struck in the statutory scheme, as delineated in the governing caselaw, petitioners have stated no legally cognizable claim to participate in the broadcast debates.

In addition, petitioners' demand for inclusion in a particular program raises "the risk of an enlargement of Government control over the content of broadcast discussion of public issues."[32] Petitioners would have the Commission forbid the networks from broadcasting a debate that excluded them.[33] While broadcasters do not have the same First Amendment journalistic freedom as newspapers, Congress and the courts have been reluctant to recognize an unlimited right of governmental interference in the affairs of broadcasters.

In rejecting First Amendment challenges by broadcasters to the statutory access scheme, the Supreme Court has consistently emphasized the narrow scope of the restrictions contested.[34] In *Columbia Broadcasting System, Inc.* v. *FCC*,[35] the Supreme Court rejected a broadcaster challenge to Section 312(a)(7),[36] which creates for candidates a limited right of reasonable access. The Court held that "the statutory right of access...properly balances the First Amendment rights of federal candidates, the public, and broadcasters."[37]

---

[32] *Columbia Broadcasting Sys.* v. *Democratic Nat'l Comm,* supra note 10, 412 U.S. at 126, 93 S.Ct. at 2098, 36 L.Ed.2d at 797.

[33] P.App. at E-5.

[34] See, e.g., *FCC* v. *League of Women Voters,* supra note 22, 468 U.S. at 380, 104 S.Ct. at 3118, 82 L.Ed.2d at 292.

[35] *Supra* note 12.

[36] 47 U.S.C. sec 312(a)(7) (1982).

[37] *Columbia Broadcasting Sys.* v. *FCC,* supra note 12, 453 U.S. at 397, 101 S.Ct. at 2830, 69 L.Ed.2d at 729.

While it emphasized that "the First Amendment 'has its fullest and most urgent application precisely to the conduct of campaigns for political office,'"[38] it underscored the restricted nature of the statutory right:

Petitioners are correct that the court has never approved a *general* right of access to the media...Nor do we do so today. Section 312(a)(7) creates a *limited* right to "reasonable" access that pertains only to legally qualified federal candidates and may be invoked by them only for the purpose of advancing their candidacies once the campaign has commenced. The Commission has stated that, in enforcing the statute, it will "provide leeway to broadcasters and not merely attempt *de novo* to determine the reasonableness of their judgments" ...[I]f the broadcasters have considered the relevant factors in good faith, the Commission will uphold their decisions...

Further, Section 312(a)(7) does not impair the discretion of broadcasters to present their views on any issue or to carry any particular type of programming.[39]

The access demanded by petitioners in this case, however, would constitute a far greater intrusion on broadcasting discretion than the carefully limited statutory access upheld by the Supreme Court in that case.

Similarly, in the seminal case upholding the constitutionality of the fairness doctrine, *Red Lion Broadcasting Co. v. FCC*,[40] the Supreme Court, while emphasizing that "it is the right of viewers and listeners, not the right of the broadcasters, which is paramount,"[41] also reiterated that "broadcasting is clearly a medium affected by a First

---

[38] *Id.*, at 396,101 S.Ct. at 2830,69 L.Ed.2d at 729, (*quoting Monitor Patriot* v. *Roy*, 401 U.S. 265,272,91 S.Ct. 621, 625, 28 L.Ed.2d 35,41 (1971).

[39] *Columbia Broadcasting Sys.* v. *FCC, supra* note 12,453 U.S. at 396-397, 101 S.Ct. at 2830,69 L.Ed.2d at 729 (emphasis in original).

[40] *Supra* note 12.

[41] 395 U.S. at 390, 89 S.Ct. at 1806, 23 L.Ed.2d at 389.

Amendment interest,"[42] and outlined the narrowness of its holding:

We need not and do not now ratify every past and future decision by the FCC with regard to programming. *There is no question here of the Commission's refusal to permit the broadcaster to carry a particular program* or to publish his own view; of a discriminatory refusal to require the licensee to broadcast certain views which have been denied access to the airwaves; of government censorship of a particular program contrary to section 326; or of the official government view dominating public broadcasting. *Such questions would raise more serious First Amendment issues.* But we do hold that the Congress and the Commission do not violate the First Amendment when they require a radio or television station to give reply time to answer personal attacks in political editorials.[43]

We recognize the importance of preserving a large measure of journalistic discretion for broadcasters as a serious First Amendment issue, and this provides additional support for our holding that the Communications Act and the broadcast access cases decided under the First Amendment do not support petitioners' claims to be included in the televised debates.

## III. THE FIRST AMENDMENT AND ACCESS TO THE BALLOT

Petitioners contend, however, that this analysis is thwarted by what they assert as a newly-emergent social fact: that participation in nationally-televised presidential and vice-presidential debates is now a prerequisite to election. They insist, therefore, that their exclusion from the debates effectively excluded them from the ballot and

---

[42] *Id.* at 386, 89 S.Ct. at 1805, 23 L.Ed.2d at 387..ls2
[43] *Id.* at 396,89 S.Ct. 1809-1810, 23 L.Ed.2d at 392-393(emphasis added)

denied voters sympathetic to their cause their First Amendment right to associate through the election and to cast their votes effectively for the candidate of their choice. They rely upon prior decisions of the Supreme Court striking down restrictions on a candidate's access to the ballot as violative of the First or Fifteenth Amendments. Petitioners' First Amendment claims thus differ from those asserted in *Columbia Broadcasting System* v. *Democratic National Committee* and the other broadcast access cases. Safeguarding the integrity of the electoral process is a fundamental task of the Constitution, and we must be keenly sensitive to signs that its validity may be impaired. Petitioners' argument, if valid, could affect the balance of First Amendment rights struck in the Communications Act, and might force a reappraisal of competing interests. We need not address questions of that sort, however, for petitioners have not demonstrated a restriction of access to the electoral process that the First Amendment proscribes.

In *Terry* v. *Adams*,[44] the Supreme Court held that a racially-exclusionary primary held by a private county political organization trespassed upon the Fifteenth Amendment.[45] Black citizens were excluded from voting in primary elections for nominations to county offices conducted by the all-white Jaybird Party. Since the winners of Jaybird Party elections typically ran without opposition in Democratic primaries and general elections,[46] black voters were effectively deprived of meaningful participation in the selection of county officials.[47] No such barrier was present in this case, where voters were not hindered in their ability to cast their votes for petitioners or otherwise take part in the electoral process merely by virtue of petitioners' exclusion from the televised debates.

In *Anderson* v. *Celebreeze*,[48] The Supreme Court discussed the First Amendment implications of restrictions upon a candidate's

---

[44] *Supra* note 8.
[45] See 345 U.S. at 469, 73 S.Ct. at 813, 97 L.Ed.2d at 1160.
[46] *Id.* at 463, 73 S.Ct. at 810-811, 97 L.Ed.2d at 1157.
[47] See *id.* at 470, 73 S.Ct. at 814, 97 L.Ed.2d at 1161.
[48] *Supra* note 7.

eligibility for listing on the ballot. The court recognized that the First Amendment right of voters to associate and to cast their votes effectively could be "heavily burdened" if candidate were to be excluded from the ballot.[49] Nevertheless, the Courts held, not all eligibility requirements established by the states impose constitutionally-suspect burdens on political suffrage.[50] The injury to First Amendment rights, the Court said, must be examined "'in a realistic light [of] the nature and extent of their impact on voters'."[51]

So scrutinized, it is immediately apparent that exclusion from the televised debates has a far lesser effect than would exclusion from the ballot. The former removes only one of the great number of avenues for candidates to gain publicity and credibility with the citizenry, while the latter drastically restricts voters' ability to choose the omitted candidate. The exclusion of petitioners from the debates did not prevent them from waging an effective campaign or deny voters the opportunity to exercise their First Amendment rights by casting their votes for petitioners. As it was, petitioners were able to gain ballot access in nineteen states, qualify for public campaign financing, and receive enough votes to finish fifth in the field of 228 presidential candidates.[52] Nor did petitioners' nonparticipation in the debates exclude them altogether from television campaigning. The fairness doctrine applied to discussion of the issues, the equal-time rule entitled them to the opportunity to match any nonexempt use of broadcast facilities by their opponents,[53] and as much as any candidate they were entitled to purchase advertising time at the lowest available rates.[54]

In *Buckley* v. *Valeo* the Supreme Court addressed an analogous

---

[49] 460 U.S. at 787, 103 S.Ct. at 1569, 75 L.Ed.2d at 536-557.

[50] See *id.* at 788, 103 S.Ct.at 1569, 75 L.Ed.2d at 557.

[51] *Id.* at786, 103 S.Ct. at 1568, 75 L.Ed.2d at 556 (*quoting Bullock* v. *Carter*, 405 U.S.l 134, 143, 92 S.Ct. 849, 856, 31 L.Ed.2d 92, 100 (1972)).

[52] Brief for Intervenors at 16-17 n.23..mb8

[53] 47 U.S.C. Sec 315(a) (1982).

[54] 47 U.S.C. Sec 315(b) (1982).

situation.[55] Standards governing eligibility for public campaign financing were challenged as an invidious discrimination against third-party candidates, and the ballot-access holdings were urged in support.[56] The Court put these decisions aside:

> These cases, however, dealt primarily with state laws requiring a candidate to satisfy certain requirements in order to have his name appear on the ballot. These were, of course, direct burdens not only on the candidate's ability to run for office but also on the voter's ability to voice preferences regarding representative government and comtemporary issues. In contrast, the denial of public financing to some Presidential candidates is not restrictive of voters' rights and less restrictive of candidates'. [The funding provision] does not prevent any candidate from getting on the ballot or any voter from casting a vote for the candidate of his choice; the inability, if any, of minor-party candidates to wage effective campaigns will derive not from lack of public funding but from their inability to raise private contributions.[57]

Petitioners' claims are functionally indistinguishable from the one found lacking in *Buckley*. Petitioners' supporters were not hindered from casting their ballots for them, nor were petitioners hobbled in waging their campaign. While their inclusion in the televised debates undoubtedly would have benefited their campaign, the Supreme Court has held that the Constitution does not demand that all candidates be subsidized to the point that all are equal in terms of financial strength and publicity.[58] *Terry* and *Anderson* were concerned with banishment of candidates and voters from the political arena, not with overcoming disadvantages in money and image frequently encountered by minor-party candidates.

We decline petitioners' invitation to embark upon the complex and hazardous task of recasting the First Amendment balance

---

[55] 424 U.S. 1, 94-96, 96 S.Ct. 612, 670-671, 46 L.Ed.2d 659, 730-731 (1976).
[56] *Id.* at 93-94, 96 S.Ct. at 670-671, 46 L.Ed.2d at 730-731.
[57] *Id.* at 94-95, 96 S.Ct. at 670-671, 46 L.Ed.2d at 730-731.
[58] *Id.* at 97-98, 96 S.Ct. at 672, 46 L.Ed.2d at 732-733.

embodied in the Communications Act and the policies of the Commission. We remain mindful that the Communications Act reconciles not only competing policy choices, but also interests of constitutional stature in constant tension with each other. While we will not turn a deaf ear to any plausible assertion of constitutional right, we must be circumspect in any effort to vindicate an alleged constitutional infraction at the expense of constitutional interests at least equally valid and compelling. In the present case, we find the First Amendment interests of candidates, broadcasters and the public adequately served by the adjustments made in the Communications Act, and perceive no basis for disturbing the Commission's denial of petitioners' complaint.

The order under review is accordingly

*Affirmed.*

# ACKNOWLEDGMENTS

The author wishes to acknowledge his thesis advisers at the University of California at Santa Cruz, Professor James O'Connor for his encouragement; and Professor Michael Rotkin, who also served as Mayor of Santa Cruz, California, 1981-82, 1985-86; Professor and author Todd Gitlin of the University of California at Berkeley; David Cole, former executive editor of *feed/back*, the *California Journalism Review*, which was published quarterly at California State University at San Francisco; Hodding Carter III, former host of PBS' nationally televised series "Inside Story," for his encouragement; Adam Hochschild of *Mother Jones* and one of the founders of the Citizens party; for inspiration derived from author Studs Terkel, author of brilliant oral histories such as *Hard Times* and *Working*, who is also one of the founders of the Citizens party; journalist and author I.F. Stone, who met with me about this project while he was a guest lecturer on the campus of U.C. Santa Cruz; Alex Cockburn of the *Nation*; Tom Wicker of the *New York Times* and Jack Nelson of the *Los Angeles Times*, who were kind enough to grant me in-depth interviews.

I also want to acknowledge publisher Jeremy P. Tarcher as a mentor to me in learning about the profession of publishing; Steven Warshaw, founder of Diablo Press for consulting with me about how to start my own publishing company; Toni Morrison and Dorothy Pasik, Palm Springs, California, for transcribing all the taped inter·views included in this book; literary agents Diane Raintree of New York; Ruth Aley of Maxwell Aley Agency, New York; Carolyn Bennett, Literary Agent and publisher of Gull Books; and literary agents Alida Allison and Roberta Rosenbaum, Palm Springs Literary Agency; Jack Tapleshay, College of the Desert, Writing Department,

Palm Desert, Ca.; Suzette Mahr of Words & Deeds for setting the type; Delta Lithograph, Valencia, California, for printing and binding the manuscript; cover artist, Willy Blumhoff, Blumhoff Design; Bea and Albert Cohen for the final proofreading and putting it into a word processor for the typesetter; and my copyright lawyer, Robert E. Gordon, of Sausalito, Ca.

I am also most grateful to Ms. Sonia Johnson who hired me to be her national press secretary during the 1984 presidential campaign; and to Janice Roter for doing a final edit of this manuscript.

I would like to acknowledge the love and belief in me that my late mother, Phyllis Gale, projected, which helped me make this book a reality.

# About the Author

Jeffrey Gale has been a journalist and national news media critic for the past 25 years. He won two consecutive Smolar national journalism awards for his reporting and has been published in the *San Francisco Chronicle*, the *Associated Press*, the *San Francisco Examiner*, *Players*, *feed/back*, *the California Journalism Review* and other publications.

He was also the subject of a profile in *feed/back, the California Journalism Review* for his work as volunteer national news media ombudsman during the 16-month-long San Quentin Six trial in Marin County, California 1975-76.

In 1984, he served as national press secretary for the Citizens party presidential candidate, Sonia Johnson, which gave him first-hand experience on the "other side" of the media fence, and which enabled him to write and compile this important compendium on the role of the media in presidential elections.

The manuscript for this book was prepared on an IBM AT personal computer and provided to the typesetter on a diskette.

Pages were typeset and designed on a Macintosh Plus™ personal computer, using Microsoft Word™ and Pagemaker™ software. An Apple LaserWriter Plus™ produced camera-ready pages which were provided to the printer.

The typeface used is Adobe Systems Incorporated's Postscript™ version of ITC Garamond®. Garamond was originally designed in the 16th century by a French typographer. It was redesigned in 1977 by Tony Stan for International Typeface Corporation.

Please send me:

$9.95 each _____

_____ Copies of BULLSHIT!  ($11.95 CAN.) _____

Include 6.5% sales tax if mailed within California _____

Include $1.50 for shipping and handling
(Please write for special bulk shipping rate.) _____

Enclose check or money order for TOTAL amount. _____

_____ ( )_____
NAME                                     PHONE

_____
ADDRESS

_____
CITY                              STATE              ZIP

_____
ADDRESS WHERE BOOKS ARE TO BE SENT IF DIFFERENT FROM ABOVE.

Mail to: BOLD HAWK PRESS, P.O. BOX 588, PALM SPRINGS, CA 92263

---

Please send me:

$9.95 each _____

_____ Copies of BULLSHIT!  ($11.95 CAN.) _____

Include 6.5% sales tax if mailed within California _____

Include $1.50 for shipping and handling
(Please write for special bulk shipping rate.) _____

Enclose check or money order for TOTAL amount. _____

_____ ( )_____
NAME                                     PHONE

_____
ADDRESS

_____
CITY                              STATE              ZIP

_____
ADDRESS WHERE BOOKS ARE TO BE SENT IF DIFFERENT FROM ABOVE.

Mail to: BOLD HAWK PRESS, P.O. BOX 588, PALM SPRINGS, CA 92263

---

Please send me:

$9.95 each _____

_____ Copies of BULLSHIT!  ($11.95 CAN.) _____

Include 6.5% sales tax if mailed within California _____

Include $1.50 for shipping and handling
(Please write for special bulk shipping rate.) _____

Enclose check or money order for TOTAL amount. _____

_____ ( )_____
NAME                                     PHONE

_____
ADDRESS

_____
CITY                              STATE              ZIP

_____
ADDRESS WHERE BOOKS ARE TO BE SENT IF DIFFERENT FROM ABOVE.

Mail to: BOLD HAWK PRESS, P.O. BOX 588, PALM SPRINGS, CA 92263